The Art of Tennis

This book is dedicated to Moneypenny

Dominic J Stevenson

The Art of
TENNIS

An Innovative Review of Tennis Highlights
2019-2021

Meyer & Meyer Sport

British Library of Cataloguing in Publication Data
A catalogue record from this book is available from the British Library

The Art of Tennis
Maidenhead: Meyer & Meyer Sport (UK) Ltd., 2022
ISBN: 978-1-78255-238-3

Aachen, Auckland, Beirut, Cairo, Cape Town, Dubai, Hägendorf, Hong Kong, Indianapolis, Maidenhead, Manila, New Delhi, Singapore, Sydney, Tehran, Vienna

Printed by Books International

Printed in the United States of America

ISBN: 978-1-78255-238-3

Email: info@m-m-sports.com

www.thesportspublisher.com

Credits
Cover and interior design: Anja Elsen
Layout: DiTech Publishing Services, www.ditechpubs.com
Cover and interior graphics: © AdobeStock
Managing editor: Elizabeth Evans
Copy editor: Sarah Tomblin, www.sarahtomblinediting.com

CONTENTS

INTRODUCTION

The Pre-Wimbledon Tune-Up /
The Third Beginning

Tuning up a musical instrument is vital if precision is to be met, if the execution of beauty is to be realised, if music is to genuinely reach inside people's hearts and heads and affect them. To succeed, a tune-up is imperative.

The grass court tournaments that take place on the hallowed lawns of England, Germany, and Mallorca provide players with the special feeling that comes with playing on the most natural but hard-to-cultivate-and-control surface of the annual tennis calendar. The tennis players – musicians with their instruments – not their opponent on the other side of the net, are ultimately in charge of their own destinies. Or at least that is how to approach things, with total belief in the music one can make, the beautiful sound emanating from a finely tuned body, eyes fixed on the prize, every step considered and calculated.

There is not long to find one's feet, the grass court season having by far the shortest run up to its major championships – Wimbledon – each year.

It comes in waves, and here is another, washing over us, two intense, magical, and wondrous weeks of tennis. With Wimbledon ever the starting point, kicking off with a peak moment in the tennis calendar, the wealth of quality viewing and inspiration is unparalleled, as is the feeling of the English summer taking the spotlight whether it rains or shines.

I hear voices, tennis experts, predicting a Rafael Nadal Wimbledon men's singles title victory this year. Not all go that way, of course not, not with a certain Mr Djokovic and a magician-like Mr Federer also present (for the twenty-first time), but surprisingly, and based on his close call last year, some find him the best shot in 2019. Most of the early shouts lean that way – towards Nadal. I think it's a leap, although I would personally love to see him grab his hat-trick of Wimbledon title wins.

① WIMBLEDON 2019

DAY 1

A First Major Upset in the Bag

There are shocks aplenty as Wimbledon returns with a 'bang!' Seeds are surely running scared after the first day's play; such has been the impact upon the supposed strongest – a good number scattered to the wind, a storm brewing, a storm delivered.

A player of the ilk of Naomi Osaka being ejected from the third major of the year by Yulia Putintseva, recent victor over her in Birmingham, stops folks in their tracks. Osaka has won two of the previous three majors. There is no escaping, whether she likes it or not; as the number two seed and ranked player she is expected to win such matches, even on a surface less than her favourite. Osaka finding herself a set down again to the wily Kazakh causes a ripple, if not yet a wave. The win is in the post. Perhaps. When it arrives thus, a space has presented itself in the draw, a shock logged.

And then Stefanos Tsitsipas saves several Thomas Fabbiano match points to get to a final set and, at the very least, prolong an early upset for another set. Catching the last embers of that match, the hopeful young Greek is unable to keep the Italian force at bay. The seeds look fragile, and everyone taking to the hallowed green turf is inspired, not just the instantly recognisable names in the draws. Only a short while later, Alexander Zverev tumbles out (after his older brother Mischa). While this might not rate the level of shock the Osaka exit does, once again, young hopes have disappeared. None of these younger players have yet proven their grass court worth. Ah! And the day-one-upset-train hath multiple wagons as the Tsitsipas defeat to Fabbiano is followed by the 15-year-old American qualifier Cori Gauff seeing off Venus Williams, one of her heroines. The 24-year age gap is an extreme rarity in the sport, further lending a huge spotlight to an already fascinating match on paper. A brutal first day for seeds and well-known faces of the game. Teenager Gauff impresses both in maturity of performance and how she carries herself. She has, indeed, learned a great deal from the Williams women.

Kid Qualifier Gauff Beats One of Williams's Heroines

When she got through qualifying and expressed her view regarding round one of the ladies' main draw, Cori Gauff had wanted to play Serena Williams. She had been drawn against Venus Williams. There is little denying it was a dream come true for the young starlet in waiting.

There's no 'I shared the court with my idol' about this girl as she pockets the match two sets to love and slays one of the biggest names of women's tennis over the past few decades, and in doing so, announcing herself on the biggest stage. This is a moment to record in the annals of Wimbledon folklore. While it may not deliver Venus to her retirement just yet, it does show the changing times. Unlike the men's game, most Grand Slam winners of the female variety are now in their twenties.

DAY 2

Testing Out the New Roof

Here is the story of the 'been and gone', with the roof being drawn over court one, showing off its shiny newness. And only two games come to pass under the roof, and it is done. None of the matches lean towards 12–12 and the new capped ending – the introduction of a final-set tie-break at Wimbledon (one of the latest changes introduced this year).

After a short delay, Donna Vekić and Alison Riske resume at 5–5 in the last set of their first-round encounter, and Riske swiftly breaks and then holds to put the roof's work to a minimum as the two women – one hunched over and gutted, the other beaming – head off into the London night to lick wounds or contemplate round two. Vekić loves grass and always seems to come alive at this time of year, piecing a run together in Nottingham each June, priming herself for what is to come. Her Wimbledon ticket is yet to be the one she wants. No deep run or otherwise this time around. The seed is shown an early exit.

The court one roof has debuted, making its first appearance at this year's main event, and there is no doubt it will witness some great scenes in the future of the tournament.

DAY 3

Gasparyan the Unlucky

Margarita Gasparyan is rather unlucky. Having a one-set lead and being at 5–5 in the second when playing Elina Svitolina is no mean feat, and the closeness of victory, accompanied by the smelling of blood and the fruits of such a win, is appreciated from all corners with a shower of praise and attention.

Having returned from terrible injuries and a year and a half away and being back at Wimbledon, getting back to a level to find a winning position against a top tenner and someone of real calibre, and then to be so unfortunately crippled by severe cramp must be a bitter pill to swallow as she has to withdraw. While initial thoughts of serious injury come to mind, she goes on to compete the following day in the doubles, indicating she was just extremely unfortunate to have had to pull out (owing to the short-term nature of the issue, which she will doubtless be grateful for in the longer term) from a winning position.

Gasparyan, surely one of the unluckiest faces to compete at this Wimbledon, may pass unremembered although she is fully deserving of praise, respect and wishes of good health for the future.

I Spy, With My Little Eye...

... something beginning with 'Box Office Thursday'. Centre Court has scarcely had a second-round match to cause the tennis fan masses to salivate the way the upcoming Nick Kyrgios versus Rafael Nadal match does. Nadal was moved from where he might ordinarily have been in the draw – for whatever reason, let's face it, a great injustice – to what turned out to be a much harder section of the draw compared with his number one career rival, Roger Federer, and now has a huge task in the shape of the wholly unpredictable young Australian wizard, Kyrgios. The match has been built up for months, unbeknownst to all, as both men have spoken in the media about one another and, while they wouldn't say it directly (or am I mistaken in this pondering?), they seem to strongly dislike one another. Kyrgios stating that Nadal is the opposite of him (and that evidently being the best reason to dislike someone), and Nadal speaking of Kyrgios's lack of respect for the sport he himself loves. Nadal also mentioned Kyrgios's education, although it seems the young Aussie lost the translation from Spanish to English and thought Nadal was referring literally to schooling. Alas, Centre Court will be bubbling, simmering, heating up even before the pair take to the court, such is the anticipation around a rematch of their 2014 fourth-round encounter (in which a teenage Kyrgios shocked Nadal and the world watching on). It is show-time come Thursday – a real treat for the early days of the tournament.

Did the match even need such a build up? It's like a late Saturday night much-anticipated and salivated-over boxing bout. Of the heavyweight variety. Two heavyweights. Trading verbal blows via the media beforehand. Okay, not quite, but almost. Nadal is a gentle soul with little intention of hurling anything even remotely vicious – except tennis ball missiles – at anyone. Two heavyweights. One winner. One takes the chance to line up in the last 32. One might rue the day, although that probably depends very much on who the winner is.

Khachanov v López

Karen Khachanov and Feliciano López are at 5–4 in the fourth set. Khachanov leads by two sets to one after López stormed through the first set. López is serving. Multiple deuces have occurred. Match points for Khachanov saved well by López. Game points that López failed to take. An almost never-ending game. A real excitement to it, one of those moments typical of the finest magic of the first week of a major tournament.

Khachanov does get his man there in the end and wins 4–6, 6–4, 7–5, 6–4. A brilliant second-round encounter. A challenge for both men. Khachanov's power and spirit seeing him past the reinvigorated López, hot on the heels of his Queen's Club victory. López didn't look like he wanted to let go of the match. At all. His determination was seen and raised by Khachanov, who will play Roberto Bautista Agut in round three. López gave a great showing, but was it his final one in the singles at Wimbledon?

The Follow-Up Outcome

Backing up a giant killing with another win would seem to be something that eludes most players in that position. The next match is a comedown. Cloud nine has taken effect, it's hard to keep feet on the ground, and many cannot overcome the next obstacle – often a player closer to one's own ranking or perhaps even lower.

Jiří Veselý, however, and Thomas Fabbiano a little while later, both backed up their round one wins (over Alexander Zverev and Stefanos Tsitsipas respectively) by reaching round three. Veselý dropped the opener and then battled to a four-set win over Pablo Cuevas. Fabbiano needed five to despatch of Croatian 40-year-old giant Ivo Karlović, fighting as ever as if his very life depended on it. His racket, released from his grip upon missing the shot that gifted the match to Fabbiano, showed his immense frustration at his (possibly last Wimbledon) match coming to an end.

Yulia Putintseva, ranked 39, didn't follow up her defeat of Naomi Osaka (seemingly a good match-up for the Kazakh player) and tumbled out to Swiss world number 81 Viktorija Golubic. But perhaps the best example of all is the composed and magnificent 15-year-old Cori Gauff, who followed up her win over heroine Venus Williams by maturely seeing off Magdaléna Rybáriková, a semi-finalist here two years earlier, 6–3, 6–3. Her astonishingly bright possibilities become further evident in backing up that first-round win with style. A wisdom beyond her years, a supportive family, and a team that looks set to share great things with their young protégée, she is lighting up Wimbledon 2019 in a way few could have foreseen. She has only just turned 15 (in March) and looks the real deal. Straight sets. Into the last 32. Boy, does giving her a wildcard for qualifying look like one of the best decisions since they handed one to Goran Ivanišević for the main draw back in 2001.

DAY 4

Barnstormer

It certainly lives up to its billing. The Centre Court visual feast everyone wants a piece of does provide concrete evidence Rafael Nadal is on a mission for a third Wimbledon crown, whether he ever attains that or not.

Unlike his usual slow start in matches, Nadal is up 3–0 after less than 10 minutes. The set is clinched 6–3 and Nick Kyrgios goes on to take the second by the same scoreline. Then both men become better at protecting their serves. The set ends in a tie-break, one of Kyrgios's areas of expertise, which both men would have known as they slowly and stubbornly, with tunnel vision, arrive at their shared destination. A big moment, as one man would then be leading 2–1, only a set from surely the triumph of the day.

Kyrgios has stated he won't change, regardless of the endless comments of others offering advice and support. Change is a leap, but evolution and personal growth don't appear to be taking place either in the talented Australian. Being stubborn won't only hinder his professional tennis career but his entire life. Today is a representation of both the best and worst of the ultimate modern tennis enigma. The game can't live with him, nor can it manage without him. The same can be said for the man himself and his relationship with tennis.

Nadal pushes ahead again by taking a tight tie-break, as one might expect, by seven points to five. He leads 2–1. It's the barnstormer of the first week. It'll be hard to top this majestic early meeting in the tournament between two players who could very easily be meeting in the final stages of any tournament without much surprise to anyone watching closely.

The Nick Kyrgios Baggage

Nick Kyrgios carries around with him more than just his rackets and a substantial bank of tennis tricks and skills. He has some serious baggage weighing him and, with it, his entire career down. Not fulfilling one's potential is not the end of the world. Just because you've been blessed, well, you don't have to do what you were made to do. Nobody can force success or performance upon anyone else. What makes the Williamses and the Federers and Nadals of the world so very special is not just how gifted they are but how they are – and have been – able to apply themselves mentally, to nurture their abilities into a complete package. Kyrgios wouldn't be the first to fail to make the most of what he has been bestowed with. As he succumbs to one of his apparent enemies, Nadal, it is hard not to ponder this and more about the Aussie's game and approach to life. Nadal takes the fourth set – and with it the match – once again on a tie-break, squeezing through a very early and tough test rather impressively – 6–3, 3–6, 7–6, 7–6.

The lack of a Kyrgios coach, probably down to his lack of desire to be told how to do things (which he may see as being told how to live his life) ensures he is missing the necessary guidance to harness his wildly impressive tennis. It doesn't need halting, just refocusing. There is no baggage handler. How can the transportation of the product – a remarkably gifted individual – get to the place it truly could and reach the heights of glory without it?

The Simon Comeback Narrowly Fails

Gilles Simon loves a good fight; feeds off it on the face of things. Losing the final at Queen's Club (to Feliciano López) less than two weeks ago stood him in good stead for such a match as today. What is a surprise is not that he was two sets down but that after fighting his way back to a final set he couldn't muster the necessary magic to push the tie over the finishing line in a way that a good number of his male French compatriots managed to do – in winning fashion. Close to the exit door, rather quickly in his second-round match against Tennys Sandgren, he couldn't go the whole hog to recovering when what would have been a memorable turnaround looked likely.

The match is played out at the same time as the match of the tournament thus far – the Kyrgios and Nadal affair over on Centre Court. Gilles Simon at his fighting best is a force to admire. On this occasion, it seems something of a shame that coming back from 2–0 down was just a tad too much to ask.

DAY 5

Kid's Play

The pure joy on the faces of youngsters Cori Gauff and – shortly after – Ugo Humbert shows a fresh side to tennis, something you don't see the same with the seasoned pros.

There's an innocence and undiluted love of the game on the features of those young folk. It hasn't been affected by money, success, sponsorship deals through the roof that carve and corrupt new versions of those players, aware that the millions thrown at them will shape their worlds, all bandwagon-jumping and milking dry the teat of success. The smiles are because they won tennis matches, and big ones at that, by playing out of their skins.

It's just a matter of time before the young players figure it out, reach the latter stages of the Grand Slams and go on to conquer (especially on the men's side – it's already happening regularly on the ladies' side of things). The youngsters have immense potential, just not the experience and self-knowledge to carry their talent over the line. That is where the older generation is still winning in the men's game. The puzzle is there for solving. The Gauff and Humbert runs this week show that the kids are more than capable. Gauff will take on Simona Halep next and Humbert has the rather colossal challenge of Novak Djokovic. Whatever happens, the future looks bright indeed.

Not A Bad Start, Miss Gauff

Forget that Cori Gauff (also known as Coco) almost lost to Polona Hercog on Centre Court. She didn't. She faced match points and came through. This was a week worth remembering, without doubt. No fluke; she'll be back in week two and she'll get bigger and better and deeper into these large tournaments, whatever happens against Simona Halep on Monday.

Polona Hercog could only ever be the villain of the piece, since everyone has fallen in love with the young American Gauff, this being the kind of fairy tale the British public gushes over. There is an absolutely insane tie-break at the end of the second set. Pure adrenaline, the nerve of this kid, as the crowd gets vocally behind her, urging her, even propelling her into a final set after she had looked to be down and out.

Gauff, wins the tie-break, taking it with a final point, a war of slices, a battle of nerve, with an incredible ousting of Hercog's brilliant tactics. Gauff had found a way. Her way. She was neutralising Hercog's game and coming out on top, even having saved two match points that went Hercog's way. A true sign of grit; an earmarked great of the future.

Just to remind readers, Gauff was 6–3, 5–1 down, on her way out of the Championships for this, the 15-year-old's first year in its main event.

Tick, tock, tick, tock. Games are passing like time, familiar and yet compelling. The final set is soon at 4–4 and we are reaching the nitty-gritty of this sporting confrontation. Part of the magic of this summer evening encounter – which once in a while seems to stop time and have everyone watching – is that before the tournament most spectators (both imminently attending the All England Club and around the globe) wouldn't have known of Polona Hercog and nor would they have known anything about American wunderkind Coco Gauff, and yet, here we are, all eyes fixed on this curious pairing, striking balls with fury and intensity, a battle of styles, of ages, of wills and of character.

Gauff gets a sniff on the Hercog serve at 5–4 up and a break here would seal the triumph; another huge brick in the very premature building of her own Wimbledon palace. Unfortunately, she isn't able to seize the day just yet. 5–5. A wonderfully and refreshingly accomplished service game follows from Gauff, and she again has the advantage. 6–5.

30–30. The finishing line again in sight. Yet another long rally with each staying present trying to outdo the other without overly committing. The youngster goes long. Game point to the patient and challenging Hercog, slicing things up for good measure, biding her time. Long from the Slovak. Deuce. Gauff now immune to Hercog's slice that worked so well earlier, matching it, the kid growing before everyone's eyes. Match point to Gauff. She takes it. Extraordinary celebratory scenes from the teenager (akin to a player winning the event – this I might add is from the player, her team, the crowd, everyone bar Hercog, of course) who goes wild, jumping, and her team almost launches itself collectively onto the court to join her. Tennis from another planet. The success is mirrored by the highest BBC television audience for this year's Wimbledon by a considerable margin.

Undeniably the comeback of the tournament. Box office TV. A name not to be forgotten in a hurry in tennis circles. It will be a while before it's etched into Wimbledon champion history, but it's there in the consciousness of those who follow the sport.

From a set and match point down, Little Miss Gauff completes a masterful turnaround. Congratulations, young enchantress!

Paire, the Prolific and Expert Mutterer

He isn't half bad at tennis, having a rather good season, in fact. Nevertheless, Benoît Paire is amazing at talking to, berating, and generally shouting at himself and anyone stood in his path (or maybe it's all just directed at himself). His monologues are entrancing for all the wrong reasons as his tennis often suffers, and the two are spiralling ever out of control.

He beats Jiří Veselý of the Czech Republic in round three today, but somehow the tennis seems to come secondary for a player who can be a different version of himself on any given day.

It's becoming a thing of legend, as much of a show as the tennis. While his fellow Frenchman Gaël Monfils has many tricks in his bag and has fun, he perhaps doesn't always achieve what he is capable of, and Paire huffs and puffs and erupts with his very own brand of human thunder and lighting. A striking figure on the tennis court, he doesn't come across as a man to mess with, furious when his tennis isn't what he deems it possible to be – he is a true enigma from whichever angle he is captured. Alienating fans at times when he appears to cease even trying to win, he is a puzzle nobody is going to figure out any time soon, least of all the man from Avignon, France, himself.

Plíšková Passes the Hsieh Su-Wei Test

Not an easy test, Karolína Plíšková has come through the Hsieh Su-Wei encounter with flying colours. Hsieh brings such a unique flurry of slice and other shots – other players rarely possess a similarly rich arsenal – leaving many a top player flummoxed and disbelieving, no solutions making themselves known, and a defeat appearing before you can comprehend the madness and beauty of her game. Hsieh, the Chinese Taipei player, is a handful (for anyone) and Plíšková further displays her credentials to win the title by winning today 6–3, 2–6, 6–4, telling the world she feels ready now. If she can consistently serve well, not feel overawed, and simply do the job at hand, she could achieve big things.

Plíšková looks to be on a mission, and while Hsieh took a set and really pushed her towards on-court problem-solving that will put Plíšková in a good mood about what is to come, the outcome seemed pre-ordained. Plíšková doesn't succumb to Hsieh's magic as some do and sticks to her guns, firing down huge serves, managing to break and neutralise the strange game spraying from Hsieh's racket.

That Hurkacz Dive

Hubert Hurkacz of Poland may have little in his armoury to match the flamboyance of Kyrgios, *par example*, but here is a tennis player who allows his tennis and only his tennis to do the talking.

There is a dive, an almost impossible get that Hurkacz reaches, winning the point and blowing the minds of everyone watching. Not just taking the oft-received lesson Djokovic loves to dish out, Hurkacz has the look of a man able to, if nothing more, make Djokovic uncomfortable.

Hurkacz follows up that world-class dive in Djokovic's last service game of the set with another to take a long rally on the second point of the tie-break and recover the mini break he'd handed to Novak on the first point of the breaker. Djokovic then double faults, somewhat unusually, and Hurkacz causes all manner of problems for the defending champion. When the Pole manages to squeeze his way through the tie-break 7–5 to level the match at one set all against the world number one, the order of proceedings seems to be somewhat rocked. Hurkacz never gets over it though, losing the next two sets with relative ease. What he has shown is that he won't just lie down and roll into the tennis abyss as many players facing Djokovic do. He was here to try to win. Not a bad showing he has given by the end. He will hope for even more next time. Watch this space …

Watch Medvedev Come Undone

Guaranteed at some stage in most matches, Daniil Medvedev will unravel, will undo himself, will allow in those demons some players have, hugging their consciousnesses, to destroy and deny him glory, to have their say. On this occasion, David Goffin is the one there to take advantage, remaining level-headed and keeping his head down, working, ploughing the land, and watching the seeds he has sown reap the rewards he has earned.

Medvedev v Goffin is a five-set thriller with ups and downs and twists and turns of fortune and score. It is 3 hours and 31 minutes long and, when calm is needed, Goffin, not Medvedev, who had led by two sets to one, comes out smiling and looking forward to his next match, on Manic Monday, in the second week of Wimbledon 2019.

DAY 6

The Serena and Andy Wimbledon Show Is on the Road

They didn't come here to cause a scene, nor did they want to want to merely play a match or two, a few sets, and see what they could do. They're both winners, born competitors, and they came to win. You must feel a little sorry for their first-round opponents in the mixed doubles event this year, Chilean Alexa Guarachi and German partner Andreas Mies, although they perhaps looked rather chuffed just to be sharing the court with such an esteemed pairing – another highly memorable occasion of Wimbledon 2019.

The new celebrity tennis pairing proved too much firepower and put their rivals under huge pressure to win in straight sets. By the time Serena Williams and Andy Murray were a set and 3–0 up in the second, it was impossible to see a change in fortunes. Nor did one arrive, and two happy and very famous bunnies headed off into the week one sunset, raring to go for the week ahead (Serena, along with Andy in the doubles, and still alive in the ladies' singles competition, too). The pair would go on to win their second-round match and come unstuck after a splendid little run in the third round to top seeds Bruno Soares and Nicole Melichar.

The Form of Konta's Life

Hot on the heels of a run to the semis in Roland Garros, where she had never got past the first round, is an eye-catching surge into the second week of Wimbledon, Johanna Konta's home major. The British crowd is driving her, along with some glorious tennis on the green lawns, chanting and willing her continuation through the draw as she beats Sloane Stephens in round three. Konta is in some form here, confident, more aware of her abilities and how to use them to hurt others than ever before.

She poses a dangerous threat to any opponent as she did in Roland Garros last month. She looked able to go all the way there and was only undone by a kid – Markéta Vondroušová – in the free-hitting form of her young life, fearing nothing, and striking gold to reach the final. Konta, with a past of not quite hitting the heights her talent suggested she might, now finds herself needing to push on and tick those unticked boxes – reach first major final, win first slam, conquer the world, etc.

The Riske Factor

Manic Monday is a magical and highly memorable treat for Grand Slam fans. It follows middle Sunday – a silent day off in which everyone pauses – as a unique day at a Grand Slam in the annual calendar.

Alison Riske putting out the new world number one Ashleigh Barty and setting up a quarter-final meeting with her American compatriot Serena Williams is a big talking point of the day. Post-win, Riske sounds delighted, and attention at the club is soon turned to Serena Williams (who beats Carla Suárez Navarro in straight sets) and then Cori Gauff, taking on Simona Halep, after Nadal records an easy win, too.

The women's quarter-final between the two American women tomorrow will prove an opportunity for both. Riske, battling through some unexpected wins at the Championships, will feel buoyed and confident when taking on Serena, still the lady of the green lawns. While you can't bet against the American seven-time champion, Riske does possess a game to cause damage and is riding a wave of results that might give her no fear.

Gauff is denied a quarter-final spot by wily Simona Halep, whose experience sees her through (Halep winning 6–3, 6–3). Nobody would have tipped Halep for the title, but now into the latter stages, she will be tough for anyone to knock out.

The first 12–12 and problem-solving (legendary) tie-break is coming closer, with the two Karolínas, Muchová and Plíšková, locking horns and shaping a showdown to be imminently highlighted in the record books as the first encounter ever to end in the updated way of things. But, at the last, Plíšková breaks for 11–10 and serves for the match. She is tamely broken to love, a total whimper, and looks to be also hoping the match will end with the special occasion 12–12 tie-break. Muchová squeezes through her own service game for 12–11. Plíšková then serves again, this time to stay in it, quickly gets to 0–40, saves two, and gets an unlucky net cord against her to lose. Muchová takes the marathon final set 13–11. No 12–12 tie-break. We wait for that. Plíšková again disappoints those who had picked her to win the ladies' event this year.

DAY 8

Collision Course

For the second time in six weeks (Nadal winning in straight sets at Roland Garros) – having not crossed paths since 2017 before it, and owing to Nadal pulling out of their scheduled match at Indian Wells in the semi-finals earlier this year – Nadal and Federer, the best of career rivals, are on a collision course to meet again, this time in the semi-finals of Wimbledon. Always the semi-finals these days, owing to their other nemesis, Novak Djokovic's lurking presence.

What is extraordinary this season is how consistent these men are. Despite persistent injury issues and the lacking confidence that accompanies that, Nadal is having a hugely impressive year, while Roger is about as lethal as can be remembered, finding ways through tournaments, always in the latter stages, and with a way of eking out results as efficiently as ever before.

The Big Three Again

The Big Three are transmitting the sensation that everyone else is surplus to requirements and should be spared, set free to return home, to holiday, to anywhere but here. This, once again, is their show, their event to battle out amongst themselves, nobody else even coming close. That's how it feels after four rounds of hugely impressive tennis, clearly showing they are from a different planet to the rest. That isn't to say nobody else is playing well, but, by Jove, Federer, Nadal, and Djokovic look supremely good, all three, beyond anybody's wildest expectations of where they'd now be.

Before the quarter-finals on Wednesday, five other men stand tall going into the day's four matches – Roberto Bautista Agut, Kei Nishikori, Guido Pella, Sam Querrey, and David Goffin. Of the four who prevail, few are willing to bet against three of them being the usual suspects. My own take is that Roberto Bautista Agut will be the one to join them and that he will, of course, be sent packing by the world number one and eventual champion here, again (heading for his fifth All England Club title), in the semi-final. As for the now anticipated Roger and Rafa match-up in the semi-final, and the pair's first SW19 meeting since their epic final in 2008, well, the world cannot wait, cannot look away, has already picked a side, and poured itself all over the match as if it were a dessert craving a sauce to make it even more appetising.

The Last Eight Ladies

The ladies' quarter-finals bring some familiar faces and something of a surprise element, too. Serena Williams wins the close-fought battle of the Americans (6–4, 4–6, 6–3) on Centre Court versus Alison Riske to reach the penultimate round and give herself a chance at the title.

Simona Halep beats Shuai Zhang in two. Coming from 4–1 down in the first set, to win 7–5, 6–1. Elina Svitolina reaches the semi-finals (beating Karolína Muchová 7–5, 6–4) for the first time and is the ultimate dark horse. Her ability has meant she was labelled as a potential Grand Slam champion many times over the past half decade. Now, having not matched that perception, she has fallen a little by the wayside, finding this moment perfect to pounce. She's playing fantastic tennis and looks the part as she did when she won the WTA Finals back in October last year.

Johanna Konta looks as composed as ever. Konta at her best seems to possess more time to do what she does than everyone else. When it flows, boy, does it flow. Konta blows hot and cold at the start and never recovers from her 4–1 lead, somewhat oddly. It isn't so much that Barbora Strýcová wins the match as Konta loses it. From that swift lead in set one, Konta tightened up, stopped playing her natural game – looking a shadow of herself, a ball of nerves and errors – that beat Petra Kvitová only a day previously. A howler of a performance by Konta will probably lead to some serious self-reflection and the consideration that she may never win a Grand Slam. She has the talent; perhaps the mental strength is where she is coming undone. It's a shame, as her nature and on-court grace make her a wonderful modern tennis player, endearing her to the British public. Strýcová takes her chance to reach a first semi-final (winning 7–5, 6–1) and Konta is left wanting.

DAY 9

Men's Quarter-Finals

David Goffin dares to break the Novak Djokovic serve in the first set of their quarter-final encounter today. There is no return from that point. As ever, we see Djokovic break straight back and then go on a run that scarcely sees Goffin win another game. Novak might be the best of all time at that – breaking back, building a head of steam. He then won 15 of the next 17 games, teaching Goffin a lesson for having broken his serve, quickly finding his most lethal of grooves.

Roberto Bautista Agut loses his first set of the Championships, but Guido Pella is unable to perform his magical *coup de grace* and get out of the seemingly impossible chains he's soon tied up in. Bautista Agut is through in four and sets a date with Djokovic for Friday.

Roger and Rafa do indeed set up the tantalising fortieth encounter of their careers, set for this Friday, by beating Kei Nishikori and Sam Querrey respectively.

Marathon Opening Games

Elina Svitolina and Simona Halep push and pull at one another from the offset. Halep serves first, and the opening game has multiple deuces, break-point chances not taken, almost 10 minutes on the clock as the pair joust. They change ends with Halep hanging on to serve by the skin of her teeth. It is a strong start to the match, a couple of 23-shot rallies, and it throws us all in at the deep end.

Game one on the Halep serve is matched by Svitolina's first service game. Another game lasting around 10 minutes as the two tussle and probe, with long exchanges as they explore the court and each other's games, seeking out weaknesses and corners to trap one another in.

Each of the first two games is 16 points. Halep does break and takes a 2–0 lead. A very competitive opening.

Oddly, after two incredibly long and close games, Halep is routinely broken to love (the first three games having taken 22 minutes) and Svitolina is right back in the first set, on serve – 1–2 – Halep easily surrendering the advantage after the mountain she had climbed. Halep then breaks again. 3–1. Back in the driver's seat. She serves again next. Twenty-eight minutes on the clock as she goes into a 30–0 lead on her serve that soon sees her to 4–1.

Since she was broken, Halep has taken control, pounced all over everything, and looked increasingly dominant, stealing away with the supreme tennis and confidence in her game. The Romanian breaks to love and will serve out the opener. Another intense tussle of a game ensues. Halep gets to set point several times. Fails to take those chances, repeatedly. Four chances are gone. The whole set is finally over after 43 minutes. A fascinating set of tennis and its scoreline of 6–1 does nothing to tell the true tale of the set. To do Svitolina justice would be to say it was mostly neck and neck and that Halep was more clinical at key moments. Svitolina has to hold her serve more easily going forwards or she won't find a way past Halep.

That Halep wins in just over 70 minutes, 6–1, 6–3, is testament to how well the Romanian is playing, and who saw that coming at the commencement of the Championships this year? In the other semi-final, Serena Williams sets another date with destiny when she comfortably despatches of the challenge of Barbora Strýcová 6–1, 6–2, wasting no time or energy whatsoever.

DAY 11

Bautista Agut Basks in Centre Court Semi but Loses in Four

Novak Djokovic is an astonishing force. However, when he starts to be pushed, when it doesn't all go his way, he still, at 32, acts up, revealing the child within, spoilt and bratty – the ugly side failing to endear him to crowds the world over, as he clearly craves.

If Novak had a little more humility to go with his athletic prowess, his skill, and incredible ability, and his undeniable place in history, he might be as adored as his chief competition in this era. Mind you, Lennon and McCartney didn't let Harrison into the Beatles main song-writing team knowing it just wasn't feasible to mess with a winning formula – to have three kings all sharing a platform equally. Nor could the fans cope with a three-headed beast leading the way. And so, it is with Roger and Rafa. They arrived first. They embedded themselves in the tennis public's collective consciousness, offering two different worlds and completing the dilemma. Novak Djokovic arriving thereafter meant there would never be a place for him. He can overtake both Roger and Rafa, but he will never be as universally adored. It's about much more than records, not to mention the intense interaction with the fans of tennis. In another era, Djokovic might have got on better. In fact, for sure. But, here and now, he is third in line (of the three) to the throne of most loved.

And so, Roberto Bautista Agut gave a good showing, stole a set off Novak, as some had predicted, but it was never going to be more than that. As Bautista Agut heads out, perhaps finally to his delayed stag do (owing to his surprise appearance in the latter stages of this Wimbledon), the only remaining players are the Big Three (the Nadal-Federer match to follow this one now). It's a predictable but never less than impressive situation.

40

Forty is played out on grass – the first between Roger Federer and Rafael Nadal for 11 years (following three consecutive finals together here between 2006 and 2008), on this surface, on these lawns.

Nobody could've known it'd be all these years later, their next meeting at Wimbledon, and that, in 2019, these two warriors would still be playing as they are, at this level. Scratch that. Even better is their tennis now, as they somehow against all odds and Father Time himself, continue to reinvent themselves and stay ahead of the perplexed pack.

In March, Nadal withdrew from the Indian Wells Masters, denying the entire world of the first Roger-Rafa meeting since 2017. And boy did we miss that. Last month, in the French Open semi-final, they finally coincided, and Nadal did what he does best there and showed Roger the door. Now, it's Federer's backyard. Both men are equally hungry, only one however will pass into the realms of another final, to play Novak Djokovic (who else?), who earlier beat first-time semi-finalist Roberto Bautista Agut in four sets.

Forty up, with a less memorable match than the last Wimbledon one they played (the classic 2008 final) – of course, for nothing could rise to that level again, with its history and attached weight – it is still a spectacle that the whole world of tennis would have observed. Their matches often carry a sense of expectation that is nearly impossible to meet, but knowing each time that it's closer to the final contest between the pair (and we won't know it until afterwards), all that's left to do is revel in the moments they share the court from opposite sides.

After saving two match points on his own serve in the fourth set, Nadal misses a break-back chance on the Federer serve as the Swiss has it on his racket for the match, hard to break as ever. Federer gets another match point – this time on his own serve – and Nadal spectacularly saves it. Deuce. Federer with match point again. Another astonishing passing shot from Rafa gets it back to deuce. Now, this is tennis as good as any of us will ever see. Federer again with match point. A fifth. This time he takes it, prevailing in four sets. No five-set thriller. More a four-set battle in which Nadal came alive at its end and failed to reach the level needed (other than in a second set that Roger quickly abandoned to conserve energy for the third set onwards) that he achieved back in 2008.

As the two men leave the court, you wonder if it isn't the final meeting between the two men at the All England Club. The level of tennis, though, is so far ahead of the players ranked fourth in the world and below it renders audiences speechless. A lack of superlatives, a bank of words that don't do it all justice, a breathlessness of wonder. Nadal might not have played his best tennis for the full four sets, and that was ultimately his undoing, but every moment shared by this pair on the global stage is an utter joy.

It was as compelling as ever, as the matador and the ballerina wrote further lines in their individual-yet-shared tales. It's a book that everybody wants to read and will for a very long time.

DAY 12

The Final Two

Barring perhaps Angelique Kerber, Simona Halep and Serena Williams are the best two female players of the last half decade. Halep has had to build up to magnificent things and learn a great deal from adversity, to fight, making up for her lack of height and a key weapon, and she has done it well. She was seated atop the ladies' rankings for around a year, winning all manner of titles along the way, and she finally grabbed her first Grand Slam title – at Roland Garros – in 2018. Serena is almost beyond introduction and her place in the history of the game is more than secure. She has won 23 majors, the last of those the Australian Open title in 2017. She then took leave to become a mother, and her return has seen fewer tournaments entered and more injury issues, yet Serena still reached the finals of the last two slams of 2018 – Wimbledon and the US Open – losing to Kerber and Naomi Osaka respectively.

It seems apt that this pair should meet in the final of a Grand Slam, all eyes fixed on the Romanian and the American, having a chance to add to their existing tallies. While Halep might not have been many people's tip, her surprisingly elegant and brutal surge through the draw has been thrilling. Despatching of players such as Svitolina as she did in the semi-final, in such a manner, sees her every inch the finalist that comes with less stress than it does for Serena. The world-famous American athlete has the weight of the world on her shoulders as she bids, yet again, for that elusive record-equalling twenty-fourth major title.

That Halep comes out so tough, ready, and playing with so few errors, hitting winners from all over – heading to a 3–0 start in eight minutes, with a double break – bodes well for her title attempt. Serena looks like she is chasing shadows, or her own tail. Ouroboros. Starting well is always important, but retaining that level is the hard part. 0–4. Serena then enters the fray having been a secondary figure for the start. She holds serve and has a pop at the Halep serve. 30–30. Brilliant shots by both women and it's deuce. Big serve, advantage Halep. Serena with some huge punching, amazing cross court missiles, and Halep holds for 5–1. Serena serving to stay in the set after only 20 minutes. She does. When Halep serves at 5–2 for the opening set the atmosphere has clearly found its density, as the audience becomes one with the match. Halep reaching shots pounded into the corners and Serena unable to get them back, meaning Halep stays ahead instead of Serena leading the charge. 40–15. Two set points. A perfect winner down the backhand wing by Serena. Halep takes the second and is only a set away from eternal glory after 26 minutes.

Expectations can be our undoing. Halep has talked this year about having a relaxed year. Something I thought seemed a little disrespectful towards the finite nature of a professional tennis career, especially when having her ability to win big things. However, that relaxed quality and lack of expectations has provided her with just the environment she needed to create something magical over this Wimbledon fortnight. The same opposing weight of immense expectation, by both herself and everyone else, seems to be what is setting Williams up for one stumble after another.

Serena erupts at 0–15 as her volley wins the point and that might signal a change in events. That accompanying primal screech is well-known. As Halep goes a break up and Williams serves again, Williams looks to lack the understanding that if you aren't in perfect shape and do not have matches under your belt you can't beat players like Kerber, Osaka, and now Halep. These players compete week in, week out, at the highest level. Turning up at a slam and expecting your legacy and your reputation to win you major titles would seem to belie comprehension of what top-level tennis requires. Is it the ultimate denial? Halep breaks again. 5–2. She will serve for the ladies' Wimbledon singles title for the first time in her career.

Simona Halep does exactly what she has over the 11 games she has already won. On serve, she does it in four points. Simona Halep sinks to the hallowed turf and looks at her team with total shock. Put simply, she played the match of her life. After all those emotions so close to the surface when finally wining Roland Garros at her third attempt (in the final) last year and, today, she just sailed through, unexpectedly, at this Grand Slam as if it were a fairy tale. Her opponent today had no answers. Halep made only three unforced errors in the entire final. Serena's wait goes on. Not only did she not turn up today, but to beat these top players is going to take tournament play outside of the Grand Slams. The more you play, the fitter you get. Look at Federer's run here and how sharp he is having played several clay court tournaments this year (unlike previous years) and how it genuinely makes a difference.

Simona Halep, Wimbledon champion. Blitzed it, blew Serena off her court. A woman who clearly appreciates her foundations as a human being and tennis player, who understands what she has and constantly works on improving as a person both on and off the court. A woman to give thoughtful, heartfelt speeches and ponder the larger scheme of things, not getting lost in her own bubble. Many have succumbed to ego and praise in a less elegant way by now, having accomplished even less than Miss Halep. For now, she is the ultimate female tennis role model, whatever anybody might say about those with more success in their banks. There is a richness in all areas of Halep's life that others are missing. A champion for the people, popular, kind, and with a smile that genuinely lit up the court as she basked in the limelight. It took less than an hour to dismantle perhaps the greatest female player ever. What a show.

DAY 13

Federer Produces Masterclass but Loses

People will focus on what Roger Federer did wrong to not harvest his ninth Wimbledon title, but I'd rather centre my attention on what a remarkable performance he put in, over five hours, still playing well at its end, pushing a player in supremely good form over the past 12 months, and the mindset, tactics, and grace of the man on court. Frankly, it was a thing of beauty, an astonishing feat. Those same people, those regarding the record books, will see that he lost, closely, and possibly remember the proximity of the great Swiss to victory. They will not ponder his age, his journey, what he is still capable of, and the never-ending fire that burns within him. He can say he never thought about breaking records, and, at the start, I believe that would have been true, but as he has pushed into the lead and has seen more records broken and the chance to do further damage and improve his already sparkling legacy, I believe it is what drives him on. If not for the records, it is simply for the love of the game. To work that hard, to hunger ever more. If nobody else did, why should he? It's a contemplation with little resolution.

The final was a museum exhibit to put all the others in the shade. In parts ugly, in others spellbinding, and with law-defying tennis it did indeed have everything, as Federer later attested. Part 48 of the pair's rivalry is a brand-new epic to add to the catalogue. For what art they did create.

As Roger gets older his hands get faster, whipping shots from all over (an onslaught like never before, attack-minded, a killer instinct that keeps him from harm against almost everyone else), his approach gets more aggressive, and his tactics (designed by his team) ever more lethal.

A Federer game plan that exploits the almost invisible weaknesses in Novak Djokovic sees a 10-minute game in which Djokovic saves multiple break points and escapes from unhurt to level at 2–2 in the opener.

Federer's intentions are as clear as the lack of baseline grass where many feet have trampled and worn it away.

There's nothing to separate the men until the tie-break. Then Djokovic goes ahead, is pegged back, Federer then pushes in front, but it's the Serb who finds a way and wins the opener taking the tie-break 7–5.

Federer then breaks Djokovic at the start of the second, jumping all over his man, holds to consolidate, and gets further break points, taking the second. 3–0 in set two after barely a moment to catch his breath. That Federer is 4–0 up before Djokovic wins his first game of the second set is unusual. It takes Roger 25 minutes to pocket the set 6–1, breaking Djokovic for the third time in set two, meaning Roger will serve first in the third set, just as he would have wanted.

This is the supreme incarnation of Federer. Even with Djokovic at world number one, something about Roger feels peerless. These performances encapsulate his soul, his entire career, his being.

At set point to Federer in the third, on the serve of Djokovic, the defending champion hits two perfect serves and then wins a short point for 5–5. At 6–5, Federer hits another brilliant passing shot and it's the longest rally of the match at 26 shots. Roger Federer is producing a masterclass. This might be the finest and all-defining moment of his entire career, right here, just weeks before he turns 38, becoming the oldest men's champion of the open era, should he win today.

To contextualise, who after over 20 years as a professional has been playing their best, as efficient, as effective, and as dangerous as they have ever been before? In what sport? In what dimension that we don't know of? It's unheard of, unheralded, impossible. Surely no other example exists.

Djokovic, once again serving to stay in the set, as he seems to always be, gets to 6–6 and another tie-break is necessary. The crowd is voicing its allegiance, mostly to Federer as, once again, he almost drowns in the adoration. They undeniably want him crowned for a ninth time. Djokovic again takes the tie-break though, and then early in the fourth set looks set to be showing Federer to the exit. Federer stands firm and it's 1–1. Now, Djokovic, revelling in serving first again is pressuring Federer's serve.

Roger doesn't waver. 2–2. The quality of the match is of the highest order. Not because they are both hitting the heights on every point, but because of what they produce in one another and the swinging pendulum, the shifting tides. The young players watching could learn a lot from this. The hard work, the hunger, the drive, and the spells woven here. While the cricket World Cup final is taking place, tennis – in another part of London town – of the finest standard is absorbing the world of tennis fans and folk.

Federer gets a break for 3–2, and the match looks like it could last all day; a real humdinger. The Swiss then holds his own serve and breaks again, finding a way into the Djokovic serve for fun now. Set four almost mirroring the second, as the third did the first. Roger breaking Novak for fun, every second set, and Novak winning the odd-numbered sets by tie-breaks.

A 35-shot rally against Federer at break point down. Federer hits a winner at the end of it. It has the crowd gasping. Shortly after, Djokovic finally breaks Federer, for the first time in the match to trail 3–5 and serve to stay in the set, which he does. Can Djokovic get the break he needs and bring up 5–5? No, Djokovic cannot, and Federer closes it out at the second time of asking and collars the set. 6–4.

A fifth set follows. At 1–2, Federer saves three break points and equalises the score. Djokovic gets to 40–0 and is then taken to deuce. He wriggles free and then breaks Federer for 4–2 in the final set. Djokovic is in the driving seat now. Federer's serve, which faced no break points for the first three and a half sets, is now becoming frailer. Is it tiredness? It looks a little that way. Djokovic is then down 15–30. Swings and roundabouts. Another momentum shift, perhaps? Deuce. Mistakes and tension. And Roger does to Novak what Novak does to everybody else by breaking straight back, and we are on serve once more. 3–4. Federer to serve. 4–4. Federer is really going for it now, drop shots, attempted return winners, pure attack. Djokovic doesn't back down and gets to 5–4, within reach of more glory. Federer will now serve to stay in it. Djokovic makes errors but manages to take it to 6–5. Federer again must serve to stay in the Championships. 6–6. We go on. No tie-break now until 12–12 in the final set. Djokovic keeps up his end of the bargain taking it to 7–6. They are into the fifth hour of the match now.

2–2, 7–7, 40–40. Federer gets to advantage and passes with pure brilliance to break and lead 8–7 in the final set. Federer will serve for a ninth Wimbledon title. And he will have thoroughly deserved it. The tennis is splendid now, as exciting as it has been all match, everyone hanging on every shot, the silence burst by noise, and then the noise hushed by the play. Puppets, string, a show to remember. Astonishing scenes.

The mark of a genius. Totally. He gets to 40–15. This is it. Match points. Two of them, the first is saved by Djokovic. Second match point … also saved. Deuce. Brilliant endurance and belief. Djokovic is a master of outlasting everyone else. If Roger Federer doesn't win this match, he may well be haunted by this for a very long time. Novak then gets a break point, a real party-pooper to the fun and games of the biased, 15,000 Centre Court throng. Djokovic breaks, having saved two match points. Coming from the brink of loss, not knowing how or when to be beaten, to surrender. 8–8.

Djokovic serves. 15–0. 30–0. Federer has lost six points in a row now. 40–0. Djokovic was completely unfazed at two match points down. 40–15. 40–30. Back comes the maestro. This is epic tennis. Federer is fighting back with all he has after being broken at the worst possible moment. Game Djokovic. 9–8. The Wimbledon Classic of the decade continues, Federer serving. 15–15. Then, it's 9–9. The tides, the waves, the shifting flow between the men. The set continues, ever gathering pace, because neither man will give up, neither man is able to let go, stubborn as they come. 10–9. Incredibly nervy scenes. Roger holds true. 10–10. 11–10 to Novak. 15–15. Soon 11–11. Two games from a deciding set tie-break to settle the men's event this year. No 12–12 final-set tie-break the whole event (in the first year of the new format) until the very last men's singles match. Pure fate. What a way to introduce the new concept. Djokovic sees himself to the tie-break, despite being 40–0 up and then facing a break point for Federer. Djokovic, the master of defence, saves it. You will never see better tennis than this, right here and now. 12–11.

Federer will serve once more to stay in it. Then … 12–12. It will be a tie-break to decide the men's singles final of 2019.

The tension is palpable, electric, things are boiling over. Djokovic 1–0. 1–1. Federer misses a half-volley pick-up and he's down 2–1 with Novak to serve the next two. Djokovic then serves at 4–3 up. 5–3. 6–3. Three match points for Djokovic (whose tie-break play today has been near immaculate, a thing normally seen from Roger) who earlier saved two against him. And he takes the title on the first. Djokovic doesn't explode with celebrations. He coolly walks to the net, shakes hands with Roger, bends down to pluck and then eat some of the Wimbledon Centre Court grass, pats the court, acknowledges the heavens, and takes his applause. He then howls and pumps himself up. While he calmly approached the net, his team and family had jumped and hugged and howled with joy.

It's the best Novak Djokovic has ever behaved, trying not to alienate and annoy a chiefly pro-Federer crowd (not a battle anyone could ever win). He pared down his usual shenanigans and on-court gamesmanship and arrogance, and it was a much more respectful and approachable and certainly watchable version of the Serb. If he were like this more often, simply playing and not reacting to everything like a pantomime dame, he might be as popular as he longs to be.

Roger Federer, meanwhile, has never beaten Rafael Nadal and Novak Djokovic at the same slam. Still. So, so close. It will smart for a while. A good long while.

Roger, dear Roger, how can you play *that* well at *that* age? People would, genuinely, like to know. A state of being perplexed remains. Win or lose, you cannot help but feel he won the day in people's hearts. To get to the end of the five hours and be so phenomenally close. At the same time, England won the cricket World Cup despite a draw *after* a (supposedly) deciding Super Over. You cannot help but feel today's Wimbledon final deserved a draw. Someone must win though, and Novak was just stronger. That is what it came down to. Physically equal, Novak, as ever, is marginally mentally stronger.

2 US HARD-COURT SWING
AUGUST 2019

The Serena Williams and Bianca Andreescu Firework Display That Wasn't to Be

Bianca Andreescu has had one hell of a week in her backyard, coming through anything but quietly, with a sense of fighting spirit that others wish could be bought, stolen, or borrowed. Serena Williams, as we've come to expect, has her name in the draw with the sole intention of picking up the trophy and anything less would be considered a failure by her and her entire team. That makes the Rogers Cup (Canadian Open) ladies final of 2019 a spectacular affair on paper and one that is also matched from the offset. An early break for Andreescu followed by a service hold puts her at 3–1 in the opening set.

However, Serena is in tears at an early forced sit-down. She has to withdraw injured. Andreescu cheers her up slightly, joking about her own injuries, having watched Serena most of her career, and what an inspiration Serena is to her and others. It makes Serena smile and lightens the mood in an arena loaded with disappointment. Andreescu thereby wins her first home Rogers Cup title, but who would want to win it this way when so much was promised of the pair's meeting? We do not always get what we anticipate.

Nadal beats Medvedev quite comfortably in the men's event.

Rublev's Big Bang

Andrey Rublev is on the comeback trail. He has the look of love, the eye of the tiger, the belly of a hungry beast, long caged, the body in shape again, and the confidence that comes with match wins.

In short, he looks ready to leave his mark on a tournament, much as he did two years ago when he reached the last 16 (aged 18) of the US Open and then followed it by managing the runner-up role in the inaugural Next Gen ATP Finals only a few months later. Here we are in the round of 16 at the Cincinnati Masters.

To 100% believe in your game and to execute your plan – as Rublev is doing today against none other than Roger Federer – takes some nerve, grit, and focus. Let us set aside that this is Roger's first tournament since his most harrowing career loss (that recent Wimbledon final). Let us try not to have that on our minds. As he might also be doing.

A handful of claps, a mere smatter of applause for Rublev (see, as on every Swiss legend's match occasion these days, the Federer Effect in all its glory). A cacophony for Federer point wins. The roof being raised. This time it's in Cincinnati, but it happens everywhere, the venue of little difference. How do players deal with that? I mean, *really*? Other players, well, who knows, but Rublev seems immune, tunnel vision, focused, and in the zone, even to use the situation to benefit, to use it against his opponent, redirecting the power, flair, and skill to the point at which it cannot be sent back his way. Put simply, when Rublev breaks again in set two (to be a set and a break up) it's clear that he's putting on a clinic against the Swiss legend, on how to take on and defeat him. On how not to be affected by the uneven support shown.

The fact that the crowd barely applauds the success of the Russian is hard not to be confused by. When will people attend events for a whole sport and not just a name (or two)? Let's be honest, he's near the end, Mr Federer, and if more players approached facing him in the way Rublev has, he might be retired earlier than would otherwise have been the case.

Just under an hour, Federer serves to stay in the match, the tournament, the whole shebang. He manages to scrape through and the crowd goes wild, hope renewed where there has been little. Rublev then successfully serves to pass into the last eight of the draw (where, incidentally, his fellow Russian Medvedev will blow him away) a day later. Today feels like the performance of the young Russian's life. A standout of the tournament, too, however the crowd felt. It's the manner of the Rublev victory that merits only positive attention. He rips Federer apart with style and panache. The kids are coming …

Kenin on a Roll

Somebody has sucked the fun out of tennis for Naomi Osaka. Where a year ago she looked like a breath of fresh air that permeated women's tennis as she bounced around and sounded like a 20-year-old, she now looks like a stressed world number one (yes, she's presently back in that spot) who has forgotten why she is doing this and simply feels weighed down by expectations, not to mention injury niggles.

With the US Open looming, the first slam where she will be defending champion, many questions surround Osaka.

Step forward Sofia Kenin who, at 20 years old, is a year younger than Osaka, having the best season of her young career so far, on the cusp of the top 20 for the first time and with a knack for knocking higher-ranked players from their perches (to name but one, she bundled Serena out at the recent French Open); she is a player with refreshing confidence, almost arrogance, and belief in her abilities, a feisty little on-court dynamo.

As concise with her off-court post-match win interviews as she is with her on-court movement and play (thoroughly efficient indeed), she is on something of a roll, as compelling a young force as perhaps anyone, and certainly one of the youngsters to watch in the latter part of the year and onwards.

Kenin is an aggressive player who constantly takes it to her opponents rather than waiting and hoping they make mistakes that can be taken advantage of. She is a terrier of a tennis player, possessing a swagger more familiar in rock 'n' roll stars. Perhaps that fierce characteristic along with the admirable design of her game – power, slice, approaches, some surprising finesse – is what sets her apart and sees her constantly improving. It's been a breakthrough year and who knows what is next. The sky might just be her limit.

Osaka withdraws injured at 2–0 down in the final set of their Cincinnati quarter-final. Kenin is building quite the head of steam.

The Kuznetsova Wrecking Ball

Like Rafael Nadal and Novak Djokovic earlier in the year at the Australian Open, Svetlana Kuznetsova has moved through this Cincinnati draw removing whatever obstacle – regardless of their own form – in a breath-taking display of living in the moment on a tennis court. Today, in the semi-final, it is Ashleigh Barty who is to succumb to the Russian blitzkrieg, on the receiving end of an unstoppable wrecking ball. Barty herself was bidding to get back to the number one spot, with Osaka going out in the previous round, and might have hoped for a dip in Kuznetsova's form this week. No such reprieve occurred as she was unable to find the answers, losing to her Russian opponent, 6–2, 6–4.

Kuznetsova will, of course, believe she can collar the title now, with confidence high and results from the week showing she can beat anybody. Only Madison Keys stands in her way now. Keys, however, would provide an immovable object to the Russian wrecking ball, remaining standing at the end, the American defeating her rival 7–5, 7–6.

En route to the final, Kuznetsova had impressively despatched Dayana Yastremska and the seeds Anastasija Sevastova, Sloane Stephens, Karolína Plíšková, and now Barty. Keys had seen to the exit of Garbiñe Muguruza, Daria Kasatkina, Simona Halep, Venus Williams, and Sofia

Kenin before her wonderfully impressive final match. Just the kind of form you seek in the weeks before a major. Madison Keys was once a runner-up in New York. Does she finally have what it takes to go all the way?

The Medvedev Electrical Surge

I

Despite picking up two runner-up trophies in the last two weeks (Opens in Washington and Canada), there's no denying that the best player in the world right now is Daniil Medvedev. He is really starting to show that. As he masterfully bags the second set in his Cincinnati Masters semi-final match against world number one Novak Djokovic and takes it to a decider, he looks to be in extraordinary form.

Consistency is the key as he appears to be a more settled version of himself, much calmer than in the past; the outbursts and madness tempered, channelled, impressively bottled, and used to his advantage rather than to help him self-combust.

Djokovic looked to have the match, as he so often does, almost in his pocket, as he rarely loses once having taken a one-set lead (regardless of format). When, with Djokovic serving first in the final set, Medvedev manages to break his rival for a second time today, he goes 2–1 up, the change of ends brings a moment's rest, and then Medvedev serves to consolidate the break (a tough ask against the irrepressible Serb). You cannot fail to be impressed when he stands tall and takes that 3–1 lead.

If Medvedev hadn't won, nobody would have batted an eyelid here. After all, he lost the recent finals in both Washington and last week's Rogers Cup Masters event in Montreal to Nick Kyrgios and Rafael Nadal respectively – two of the finest players on the planet on their days, and this is Mr Djokovic, winner of 16 slams, 33 Masters titles, and the world number one. So, nobody would have held it against the Russian if he had faded away in the final set – which he isn't doing.

As Zverev falters at every hurdle and Tsitsipas is experiencing a lull for the first time since his remarkable ascent to near the top of men's tennis, as Kyrgios blows hot and cold in increasingly frustrating fashion, Medvedev is the younger player now capitalising on a whiff of an opportunity to do something of substance, etching his name into everyone's mind, as we approach the final slam of the year. If this recent workload hasn't worn him out, he will believe in himself going into New York.

Djokovic holds (he was never going to be broken twice on the trot), and the pressure goes back on to the Russian, ramping up a notch even, 3–2 up, as he has to hold each time, batting away the inevitable Djokovic charge of pressure, to edge ever closer to what could only be considered one of the wins of his career, not to mention going into his third consecutive final in three weeks (and a second Masters final in two weeks – his first two ever). Marked progress, indeed. As others wane, the Russian is taking advantage of a window of opportunity, beating almost everyone put in front of him, including his two impressive compatriots Karen Khachanov (at the recent Rogers Cup) and Andrey Rublev (who earlier in the week had himself despatched of Roger Federer in straight sets). Medvedev had seen both coming, found he could quiet their styles, and won those matches well.

Medvedev may end this week fifth in the world – once more his highest-ranking spot as he surges up to the top. Imagine the confidence as we head to New York for the year's final Grand Slam in a week's time, his hard work paying off. A narrow second hold follows and it's now 4–2 to Medvedev. Two games away from an upset, a win, a real cause for Russian delight.

Moments later, Medvedev displays a steel akin to his on-court foe today and the other active greats of the game, as he extends the gap once more to two games, holding serve again for 5–3. Djokovic will serve to stay in it. Medvedev will have two games here to try to complete a massive win, stunning the crowd and shocking the expectations of many, if not quite breaking the computer systems around the tennis world.

Djokovic, as might be expected, looks a little surprised himself. It's 15–30, Medvedev not needing an invitation to go for it, to finish it here. The Serb looks rattled, without answers, and edgy, knowing he is on the ropes here. Medvedev continues the aggression, almost passes Djokovic at the net, the Serb getting to the ball and watching it tamely sink into the net. A first match point arises, Medvedev hits a clean winner to spectacularly complete the comeback, the turnaround, and break to win the match 3–6, 6–3, 6–3 (breaking Nole three times by the end of the match). A magical performance from the Russian wizard. While he should perhaps be a little tired after his recent exploits, he looks like he is just getting started. He claims the scalp of the world number one and will face David Goffin in the Cincinnati Masters final tomorrow. Neither has ever won one of these Masters Series 1000 titles before, so it'll be a first for someone. Big day. You can't help but feel it's third time lucky for Medvedev, and that, crucially, he's learned a lot from those two recent final losses.

Medvedev participates in no wild celebrations as the victory today is sealed; just calmly looks over at his camp as if it say, 'I told you I could beat him' or just possibly, 'We did it, just as planned!' There's a final still to play and, if he does win it, you can't help but think, right now, he's also the hardest working player on earth as well as the one in the best form. What a year for the young Russian. Going from good to better and beyond, locked inside the top 10 and heading to the ATP Finals in London this November.

II

The following day it is indeed third time lucky when Medvedev beats David Goffin in straight sets – 7–6, 6–4 – to claim the first of what will probably become a lovely collection of Masters titles for the Russian. While the format is obviously different at the Grand Slams, he is surely one of the key players to watch there outside of the usual three gents.

It's a shame, however, that for the men's showpiece (as the match draws to a close) more than half the stadium is empty, seats calling to be filled, open-mouth seats salivating for an audience for this elite-level tennis. If the top three aren't in action it seems 'tennis' fans aren't remotely interested in the sport at all, not there for its soul and the other important and impressive players.

Medvedev tries to hurry to serve out the match and gets caught out to face two break-back points, which he duly saves. Not before he throws his racket at the ground in a moment's frustration, perhaps his Mr Hyde (opposite of Dr Jekyll) character is never far from making its presence known. He closes out his first Masters victory to a near empty arena, which doesn't seem to be as satisfied with this winner as it was with homegrown Keys winning the ladies' several hours earlier. Medvedev thoroughly deserved this title. Exciting times looming for the young Russian.

3   US OPEN 2019

Rublev and Tsitsipas in Round One Banquet

When two players of this ilk find the other blocking their path this early in a Grand Slam (round one), they probably feel a little frustrated. As spectators, we all know the draw is strong. You might even say both players are a little unlucky as any tournament would benefit from having both in the latter rounds. It's the way of things with unseeded players returning from injury (Andrey Rublev here) or poor form and moving back up the rankings – they naturally get pitted against those they would normally be kept apart from until at least round three (the seeded Stefanos Tsitsipas here).

The calibre of opposition for each young man this early makes for a potential humdinger of a match, something the fans can get their teeth into, an early surprise, a banquet for sure. And it is, from the very off. Rublev breaks immediately and soon faces two break-back points – at 3–2 up – for Tsitsipas to get back on equal terms. Rublev remains steady and keeps his nose in front, 4–2. Meanwhile, on the other courts, Petra Kvitová and Belinda Bencic are up a break in the first set of their matches with Denisa Šátralová (née Allertová) and Mandy Minella respectively, Jeļena Ostapenko (v Aleksandra Krunić) is on serve and Roberto Bautista Agut is close to collaring the first set in his opening round match against Mikhail Kukushkin.

Andrey Rublev is fixated on his mission, ploughing the field of desire to take a scalp today and reach round two at Flushing Meadows (the scene of his best Grand Slam result so far – his run to the quarter-finals here two years ago, in 2017). Rublev, courting another notable victory in the famous American city today, stays cool and serves out the opener 6–4.

At the exact same time, according to my simultaneous Eurosport streams, Kvitová and Rublev walk towards their chairs in their respective matches, a set to the good, a step closer to round two (as too are Bencic, Bautista Agut, and Ostapenko).

Rublev presses on and breaks first in the second set. Serving at 2–1 he is soon at 0–30. His, at times, grade one tennis is waving its magic wand, unsettling Tsitsipas, who is starting to get angry and talk to himself again. Tsitsipas is struggling to find any kind of rhythm, until Rublev plays a messy game, and a break back makes it all level in the set again. It feels more about Rublev at this stage and that his play will determine the outcome here today.

Bencic wins in two, sailing into the next round. Bautista Agut loses the second set to Kukushkin, making things square. Ostapenko is a break down and soon claws her way back to take the second set to a tie-break, which she wins, sealing her victory 6–3, 7–6. Moments before Ostapenko won, Kvitová also went through.

Rublev and Tsitsipas head for a tie-break to decide their own second set. Tsitsipas leads 4–2 at the change of ends and doesn't falter. He draws the match level and it's all to play for – a thrilling match for the most part. As our two protagonists enter a third set, elsewhere Bautista Agut falls a set behind and now has a real task to turn the tables back on the ascending Kukushkin.

Meanwhile, Rublev gets the third-set breakthrough and leads 4–2. It is a lead that doesn't last as his serve is immediately broken and then, for whatever reason, Tsitsipas is unfathomably allowed to leave the court midway through the set at 4–3 to Rublev, and mid-game. No excuse is forthcoming, nobody has a clue what is happening, and his niggles have turned into full-blown gamesmanship. What else could you call this?

Rublev wanders around the baseline pondering the same as many of us (no?) – how is his opponent allowed to just depart the court? Hard not to agree it's a bizarre turn of events. Tsitsipas is off court for over five minutes. No excuses, no apologies, nothing being done about it. Umpires need to apply the rules. Consistently. This is a strange showcase of player power, an ugly side of the game, and it is in fact cheating. And the match dynamic is altered, the mood unnecessarily darkened.

Bautista Agut storms back in the fourth and soon pockets it by a 6–3 margin, taking the match to a deciding set. He gets the first break of serve in the final set with a valuable lead and it's the first time the Spaniard has been ahead in the match since the early stages.

It's soon 5–5 in the third of our Rublev – Tsitsipas match, heading for and then reaching another tie-break to separate our Greek and our Russian and give someone a splendid lead. An epic tie-break ensues. It feels like a big moment in the context of the match. Both men have set points on their own rackets, neither taking their first opportunity though.

Back with Bautista Agut, he has been broken back and it's two apiece in the final set.

In the end, Rublev takes the breaker, mini-breaking Tsitsipas and then serving to capture what feels like a vital third set for him (9–7 in the tie-break). Tsitsipas then sees a trainer as if to say that is why he lost the set. It's all happening. Tsitsipas is up to tricks that entertain for all the wrong reasons.

Bautista Agut goes on to lose in five to Kukushkin in a real topsy-turvy affair.

Opportunities to break in set four come and go, until finally at 3–3 Rublev breaks Tsitsipas on his fourth break point of the game. Rublev is a break up, a mere two games from the win now. And what a win it would be for him.

Tsitsipas then has a meltdown. It cannot be deemed age-related as many others his age do not behave in such petulant and match-spoiling fashion. You can learn a lot about a person by how they approach their job. And … Tsitsipas then gets a time violation and he is docked a point. He's his own worst enemy here. And what on earth is he thinking?

What exactly is the strategy and why is there such little respect displayed for the authorities and for all others involved in the sport?

Rublev holds serve. 5–3. A game away from a huge win in the first round. Tsitsipas then holds to love but he has given a terrible account of himself today. It's all too often that his bad behaviour overshadows his undeniably special tennis. Rublev serves for the match and is duly broken. Rublev then breaks again. 6–5. He will serve for a slice of cool justice here in a few moments … And this time, the Russian does indeed seal a brilliant victory, beating the number eight seed Tsitsipas 6–4, 6–7, 7–6, 7–5.

The crowd is totally unable to see Tsitsipas' shenanigans, gushing over him as it does, and it's a shame character means nothing to many tennis fans, who strangely pick and choose what to get irate about and what to instantaneously overlook. They seem to pick their player, and nothing makes them waver in their belief. A sign of the times, perhaps.

It's some appalling on-court behaviour, and the match shows the best (or at least a glimmer of it) and the worst of the young Greek star. Let's hope Tsitsipas soon gets his head down and stops the toying and the gamesmanship and just plays tennis, with a dose of respect and an awareness of his surroundings. *Dear Stefanos, others matter too.* Where is the compassion towards them? This isn't a good look for the sport and if anything, the issue is ballooning.

But this is the day of Andrey Rublev, back in New York and playing some wonderful tennis. Who knows where he goes to next from here?

DAY 3

Rainy Day

When the rains come; when it all stops except in the grand stadiums with roofs, and for those lucky punters seated therein.

The hard blue courts flooded. The watchful eyes of those working at Flushing Meadows. Eyes to the sky. Hopeful of live action. Predictions of widespread play later thwarted. The sky still unleashes its army of droplets, rain as far as can be found. A washout.

And the rain means more matches for the following day, an overflowing cup, the matches spilled all over the floor. Time to catch up, to swamp the courts with matches, to provide a New York-style feast that will make up for the rainy day gone before and the need to sit and wait, as everyone involved has had to.

DAY 4

The Hyeon Chung Magic Trick

Hyeon Chung has something up his sleeve. Remember his run at the 2018 Australian Open? Remember how he was foiled by both injury and the rather lofty target of Roger Federer (hard to play when fully fit let alone with a handicap) at the site of Federer's last (ever?) major triumph? We have not seen much of the wonderfully spirited competitor from South Korea since.

Chung excels over the five-set format in his second-round match today. The comeback against Fernando Verdasco from two-sets-to-love will be memorable to many. Those first two sets were not even close and then, somehow, despite almost being ushered out several times between the end of set three and the end of the match, Chung came through, with a magical performance, the final score reading 1–6, 2–6, 7–5, 6–3, 7–6. A phenomenal performance of grit and determination showing if his body is in the right state, he is a match for anyone. Whether he will be recovered in time to take on the challenge of Rafael Nadal in round three remains to be seen.

Zverev v Tiafoe

This was as it should be between the young players – a match about tennis. The hug between Alexander (Sascha) Zverev and Frances Tiafoe at the end of a well-contested five-set match between the young pair was a signal of mutual respect and appreciation.

No shenanigans. No gamesmanship filter applied. Just an up and down match in which neither player seemed to have a hot streak at the same time as the other.

Zverev won the odd-numbered sets, and Tiafoe the ones in between. That can only mean one thing: the German will line up in the third round, while Tiafoe, once again, will head off to consider how he often comes close but never quite gets the run together that we hope for. At their best, both men are highly watchable, but Tiafoe has something you can't help but want more of.

DAY 6

Saturday Night Fever

In a couple of hot late-night feasts, Arthur Ashe stadium was party to – and a party because of – some monumental tennis.

The Americans were in loud voice to oversee their wunderkind, 15-year-old Cori Gauff ('Coco' – check out the team's smashing t-shirts and Gauff's trainers), take on defending champion Naomi Osaka in a thrilling ride of tick-tock groundstroke tennis. The crowd was treated to something great. Osaka flew into a 3–0 lead only to be broken back for 3–2.

At that point, Osaka breaks again and at 4–2 up looks in control once more. As Gauff gets to break point again on the Osaka serve, the Japanese player unleashes her knowing smirk as if to express her frustration with cynicism. She is then broken as the net cord intervenes and then sends her ball wide. Back on service. 3–4. Gauff to serve next. Gauff is suffering on serve, all the anxiety spilling out, arms and limbs tight, tense, mistake laden. Another break and Osaka, at 5–3, is in touching distance of the first set. She serves for the opener. Osaka, in the cauldron here, is rattled too. Things are electric in Arthur Ashe stadium. The two-time Grand Slam champion stays cool for the set. 6–3. Gauff a little unfortunate there.

Gauff then self-destructs with multiple nervy double faults revealing her age (the very epitome of youth) and inexperience of the grand stage. Nobody can be disappointed in her for that. Gauff then gets three immediate break-back points, not without her own opportunities in this match, too, only failing to take many of her own, or being able to then consolidate when she does get the break (see set one). Osaka saves all three points. Is that the key damage, the door slamming shut in the youngster's face? 6–3, 2–0 to Osaka. Gauff with a Japanese mountain to climb now.

If a serve and its stability bring a player some control and routine, then it's a source of many of Gauff's problems now as she is freefalling. It's a tentative shot, a vehicle breaking down, not getting (her) to where it should be, revealing her tender years and vulnerability at this level, in turn adding further pressure to her groundstrokes. It feels like a meltdown but it's quite possibly just a little too much too soon. If it wasn't a 15-year-old that we were watching here it might be more worrying. She slips deeper into the abyss, 3–0 down and looking almost tearful, staring down the barrel of Osaka's gun and, rather disappointed, let down by herself on one of the sport's biggest stages. Three turns into 4, then 5, and Osaka serves out for a 6–3, 6–0 win. In the end, it wasn't what people had hoped for even if it was a spectacle. Six years her opponent's senior, Osaka just knows how to get the job done. Osaka being very tight with her young rival, offering nothing in the second set, snapping it all up, hungry for more Flushing Meadows glory. Osaka gives Gauff nothing but a lesson in how to keep your cool. One hour and six minutes and *c'est finit*. School is out. The kid, Gauff, making Osaka seem like a stalwart, is interviewed afterwards, Osaka sharing the spotlight with her young colleague. Both girls are teary, and it's been a strange but wonderful match, albeit a short one. For Gauff, it's a hard lesson to learn, but one that will contribute to making a very, very special player in the not-too-distant-future. I mean, she's already got the necessary tools and then some; it just takes a little time and patience to piece it all together. The interviews with the pair are revealing and unique. A window into both young women's worlds.

Rublev v Kyrgios follows and, in what could be very much a display of serving superiority, the match does indeed begin that way. Short, snappy points, neither man wanting to mess around and be held to ransom on serve. Rublev serves first. 2–1. Kyrgios's serve looks utterly impossible to return as he wins his second service game to love in mere seconds. So, it's going to be like that then. 2–2. Only seven minutes on the match clock. Kyrgios starts to grumble (predictably), toys fly out of his pram. 4–3 to Rublev. On serve. Is spending the whole changeover moaning to the umpire over everything and nothing (Kyrgios here) a decent use of down time? Everyone knows the answer. Except for Mr Kyrgios.

You have to feel sorry for Andrey Rublev (almost a bystander in the Kyrgios Show). The Russian is there to work. To play tennis and to fight. He has the same conditions to play in as Kyrgios. Kyrgios, as Tsitsipas did in round one, is just doing everything on earth to disrupt his opponent's rhythm. If Kyrgios is annoyed because of Rublev's style, well, it's ironic as he plays a similarly fiery style of explosive serving and huge, decisive groundstrokes. The complaints continue again at the next changeover; this time that he cannot see the ball owing to the bright lights.

Two consecutive Kyrgios drop shots fail and it's 0–30, at 4–5 in the opener. Danger averted. 5–5. On serve still. 6–5 Rublev, moments later. Kyrgios then bags his service game in 43 seconds and it's time for …

(drum roll, please) a first-set tie-break. Rublev gets things started. Kyrgios fails on the return. 1–0. 2–0 as Kyrgios hits a shot into the net. Ace. 2–1. Rublev more focused. Clinical. 3–1 he leads. Kyrgios's endless muttering is hurting him, whether he knows it or not. 4–1. For the Aussie, all to play for. Kyrgios too casual at the net and misses an easy volley. 5–1. Big serve. 5–2. Comeback? 5–3. 6–3. Three set points to the Russian. 6–4. The American crowd clearly adores Kyrgios. Rublev *just* edges the set 7–5 in the breaker. Deservedly.

If Kyrgios 'can't see a thing' as he keeps stating, then he's doing one hell of a job out there. He needs to zip it and just play, as we all know he can. His concentration is like that of a small child in a toy shop.

Both men trade break points. None is taken. It's soon Kyrgios up 4–3 in the second set. The set looks headed for another tie-break despite Kyrgios drawling – as with all his comments, at the top of his voice – he doesn't 'want to be here'. It's a charged comment and not very well thought out. It's just a typical day in Kyrgios-land. Everyone seems to either ignore or revel in his on-court madness. A second breaker it is. Kyrgios soon has a 2–0 lead in it. 3–0. 4–0 becomes 4–3. Concentration dips. All square. 5–4 to Kyrgios. 5–5. Brilliant effort from Rublev to draw back. 5–6 as Kyrgios serves to stay in the second set and Rublev again wins it 7–5. The journey to get there was rather different, same scoreline. Kyrgios again lost his focus. Under 90 minutes on the clock after two compelling sets.

Kyrgios, down two sets to love, is bound to feel aggrieved and fed up. The break that didn't come before arrives in the third, and at 5–3, Rublev will serve to be in the next round, with a raucous crowd against him as they want the match to be kept alive. 15–15. Two-punch move and it's 30–15. Kyrgios goes long. 40–15. Two match points. A brilliant win for Rublev is sealed and he once again shows that he can stay focused while the other player self-combusts.

Rublev's post-match interview smile says it all. It just means more. His mentality and match philosophy are great, and he is just happy to be back, injury-free, and playing so well. He's going to be tough to beat. Humble and a thoroughly decent guy, it's lovely to watch Andrey swing.

Wozniacki Fails to Contain Andreescu's Wild Majesty

Bianca Andreescu moves into her secret gear, the one that has had top players running scared this year. She is a fearsome tennis fairground attraction.

Andreescu can hit a beautiful and well-disguised drop shot. At 0–15 in game eight, with Caroline Wozniacki leading 4–3, Andreescu serves and, when the ball comes back, she hits an unreachable soft pillow of a shot. It's sublime, and a further reminder that Andreescu is anything but all about the power. The ladies are genuinely probing one another, seeing what is possible, moving each other around the court and trying to outhit, outmanoeuvre, and outthink.

At the changeover, after Andreescu serves out the first set 6–4, Wozniacki takes a medical time-out to deal with an ankle issue. She appeared to roll it slightly moments earlier. That's the kind of effect Andreescu's incredibly powerful and fearless game has on opponents. She is a bulldozer leaving her mark everywhere she goes.

The medical time-out simply informed Andreescu there was something to pounce all over. And pounce she did. She didn't need the invitation in the first place. She has a 'no mercy' approach. Attack, attack, show no clemency for a wounded animal. And attack she does. Less in waves than in constant punches. And before long, Wozniacki is a set and 3–0 down. The insult added. Then, oddly, it becomes 3–3. Level again. A let-up. Relief for a moment. Then … Andreescu breaks again. As does Wozniacki, clinging on, fighting for an impossible escape.

And then it's over. Andreescu breaks and soon storms into round four, the last 16, 6–4, 6–4.

DAY 7

Djokovic Crumbles, Wawrinka Pulsates

Before this event, Novak Djokovic had won four of the last five Grand Slams, only Rafael Nadal providing a blemish on the record of the Serb as he strode his way back to world number one, leaving a trail of destruction in his wake.

Enter Stanislas Wawrinka. Known to depose those at the very peak of the tree. A nemesis for Djokovic if ever he had one. While Novak has won most of their encounters, in recent years Wawrinka has brought his A-game to their Grand Slam encounters and either won or come close. Wawrinka is the player with the least fear of the Serb. If anything, he likes playing him and is astutely aware he can better him, Novak drawing Stan's finest tennis from his pouch.

Wawrinka's holy grail of a backhand is in stunning working order today and scarcely breaks down provides the source of great magic in the pair's contest, splicing and spraying itself all over the court, demolishing Djokovic as he does others. The shoe is certainly on the other foot. Well and truly.

And for Wawrinka – who spent a great deal of time injured following his US Open win in 2016 and has had to slowly work his way back to form, back up the rankings, back to these positions – it has not been easy. Yet still, who saw this coming? Despite Wawrinka's power over the Serb – and for sure nobody else holds this – who could have foreseen such a gutsy and special performance? As Djokovic crumbles, Wawrinka pulsates, blossoms, electrifies. As Djokovic caves, Wawrinka excels. As Djokovic flunks out, Wawrinka sails through with flying colours. Passing, indeed.

On today's showing, this is the kind of form that has brought Wawrinka three major titles. He's that good again. This is the 'Wawrinka Factor', and the crowd clearly wants to see more, going wild for him, Stan knowing exactly how to play up to them, to feed their hunger. It's a hothouse atmosphere indeed. The crowd throbs, coming in waves, buoyed as Wawrinka breaks in set two for the chance to serve the set out and takes a 2–0 lead in the match. This is huge, and the eruption of cheers, applause and general excitement is in accordance with what is being witnessed. Unbreakable Djokovic looks to be heading out. 6–4, 7–5.

And there is poetry. Of the pretty kind. Wawrinka's backhand is a thing of spellbinding beauty, surely one of the shots of the tournament. And Roger Federer will be watching (perhaps), and Rafael Nadal will be watching (possibly), and those men will know that with Djokovic gone from the draw, here is a rare opportunity to add to their overall tallies of Grand Slams. Wawrinka would also be in with a shot in this kind of mood.

Djokovic hands a love service game break to Wawrinka for 2–1 to the Swiss in set three and calls it quits, seemingly injured. He would later detail he'd been carrying a shoulder injury for several weeks; Djokovic is not one for losing or taking it well. It's a strange ending, Djokovic even being booed as he leaves the court. The Serb knew Wawrinka had his number today – Novak far the inferior player. It's a happy day for Stan the Man, the crowd, and Roger and Rafa, make no mistake whatsoever about that.

Post-match interview, Stan states it's been two years to get back to this level. And he is. He really is. This is exactly how he won three years ago.

DAY 8

The Set Nobody Wants to Win

When Julia Görges took on Donna Vekić, who could have known that it would be more a tale of nobody wanting to win than the reverse. A first-set tie-break with almost endless mistakes, gifts, and frustration.

A few brilliant shots from Görges are ultimately the telling difference. While you want to see a concentrated form of a player's best bits in a tie-break, it can also be when they crumble, they break, and they bow.

The *set* nobody wants to win – or is able to seize – turns a little into the *match* nobody wants to win. Errors rule supreme, and neither woman takes the match by its throat. It is more lost than it is won. Of course – both women want to win. It just doesn't 'feel' that way at times. Görges is a break up in each set. In the first, she manages to scrape through in a tie-break and, from such a commanding position in the second set, breathing down on Vekić for the match, she ends up inside a third and deciding set. Each player is more afraid of losing and not getting into the last eight at Flushing Meadows rather than positively going for it and ensuring glory.

Görges should absolutely have won this match in straight sets. That she ends up on the losing side can only be deemed her own fault. When Vekić breaks for 5–3 in the final set it might appear to some to be over. But in this match, anything is possible; another break, and Görges has chances to break back and save the match, but she fails. A day for rued opportunities. A match that wanted to hang around. Vekić, in the end, did well to turn it around, hang in there patiently and subject Görges to a damaging loss. I mean, really, how often do such chances to reach a Grand Slam quarter-final come around for most players?

Trading Blows

The exchange of explosive baseline groundstrokes, the pulverising punches as balls whizz off rackets are tigerishly eyed, hunted down like lost dreams. The sweat pouring, the t-shirts soaked, sticking to athletic bodies, the glistening arms and legs, the interactive audience, a part of the match canvas, a miniature control room affecting the outcome.

Ball on racket cracks like a whip. Repeatedly and yet never monotonous. Vicious arrows, splitting the spectators, ripping holes through the air. The lengthy rallies, the patience, the life inside every point, the ability to outlast, outshine, outcompete.

Blow upon blow landing, looking for the vital one to connect, to sink the foe, a distant ship vanishing from view, magnetised to, destined for, drifting down toward the seabed.

*I had let the matches warm up and now they were as hot as hell. Freshly served dishes from the oven. Diego Schwartzman sees Alexander Zverev to the exit in four sets, coming back from a set down, making it about tennis and not the (supposedly) defining quality Schwartzman possesses that the media always seems to focus on.

DAY 9

Match of the Tournament

When Grigor Dimitrov squeezed out the fourth set (in their quarter-final) taking his match with Roger Federer to a decider, there was no doubt whatsoever that this was the highlight and potential shock of the tournament so far – for how engaged and electrified the crowd was; for the hunger and quality of the mirror-like shot-making styles; for the ebbs and flows of the encounter. Late night entertainment on Arthur Ashe court.

Two sets all. Roger then leaves the court to change his clothes. Or to recalibrate his mind somehow. Then he leaves the court again, only this time with a physio, to receive a medical time-out. What this must do to Dimitrov's concentration as he is left alone on the court with his thoughts remains to be seem – sometimes it is certainly a tactical approach by the player causing the interruption, although who can ever know for sure (this time it is a genuine injury). It's a chance to exercise, stretch his limbs and reset for what is to come, and Dimitrov retains his focus well.

Many do not doubt that Federer will blow out the Dimitrov candle routinely upon the resumption – injury or no injury. That is no reflection on Dimitrov, his abilities, and the way he is performing today. It's only ever about Roger Federer and his superpowers.

However, another script has been ignored. Stunned faces, muted voices, numbed sensations follow. As Federer is broken and Dimitrov holds for 2–0 in the final set, confusion reigns supreme. Is this the end of the number three seed, the master, Federer? Something is not right. The public has no knowledge of any injury. Federer's cards are on his chest. No awareness of a previous issue for anyone. Something is going on here. Federer is now missing all kinds of standard shots, well within his wheelhouse. A Federer double fault – unusual in itself – occurs and Dimitrov has break point. For a double break. This is unheard of. Shock reverberates around the stands. This wasn't meant to happen. Silence emerges as words and their sounds are swallowed in constricting throats. With Djokovic out, the way had been paved for the elusive Nadal v Federer match at the US Open that has never happened before. Alas, it was not to be. Time is ticking, running out the door. Nobody cares about the other names (and faces and their abilities and personalities) left in the draw. Nobody really cares. It's always been about these two, and this is yet another blow.

Dimitrov to serve. 3–0. Here we go … if Federer is injured then it is affecting proceedings. But there's no denying that Dimitrov has earned this victory should he close it out and is in the form of his life post-injury. Boy, does being away from the court lend to finding a new perspective on things, bringing a renewed love, desire, and appreciation of how they make a living, of what they do.

First Djokovic falls, and in the next round Federer tumbles out after him, too. What a comeback, Grigor Dimitrov. You still had to take it, to grab that opportunity. A semi-final awaits the Bulgarian.

One of the Oddest Sets Ever

Medvedev v Wawrinka kicked off with one odd set in their quarter-final in New York. It happened thusly …

Medvedev breaks Wawrinka's serve in game one. From a stack of Medvedev double faults to missed chances for Wawrinka, Medvedev holds serve. The set then proceeds on serve, business-like. Medvedev is injured though, has his leg taped. His movement is restricted, so he has the tape removed. His movement is set free again. Wawrinka breaks back as Medvedev looks unable to move properly. A tie-break looms, arrives, doesn't quite dazzle. A lot to take in for just a set. Medvedev takes the breaker by eight points to six.

The set feels like the highs and lows of Daniil Medvedev's tennis, for none of his shenanigans and bad boy behaviour are produced from his kit bag today. He is focused and in that other zone. Without his chuntering and general craziness, he is a lovable guy, or perhaps it is because of that, *à la* Andy Murray. Despite the weird goings-on, he remained impressively calm. He would later state that for the first two sets he was close to retiring. He ended up two sets up and saw it out from there in four. A wonderful win. He will face Grigor Dimitrov in the first Grand Slam semi-final of the Russian's career. Dimitrov has previously lost in the semis at both Wimbledon (2014) and the Australian Open (2017). He earlier conquered Federer in a brilliant five-setter.

DAY 10

Five Sets, Please

Show us where we are, please, post us to five-set heaven, give it all to us. It could only be a major. It could only feel like our very lives are on the line. Here. The stakes are high. Here, where it is all up for grabs.

As Matteo Berrettini won the second set to level in his quarter-final match with Gaël Monfils it looked, smelled, and felt like it'd go the distance. A five-set match written all over it. The tides of tennis coming in waves for one man and then the other. If tennis was graffiti, then this match was to be a sprawling mural covering a tower block or underground passageway with endless colour (playing) and character.

And just as Berrettini had levelled at a set all, Monfils did so to make it two apiece, with Berrettini having got his nose in front by winning the third set. Therefore, it was indeed a final-set duel, which fittingly came down to a tie-break. The penalty shoot-out of tennis. A fair ending? What is fair after almost four hours on court. After all that work and then a race to seven points that leaves one player left wanting, right at the close.

Monfils has been in a couple of slam semis, Berrettini has gone from strength to strength this year, his undeniable breakthrough season, but he has not been in this territory before. Berrettini commenced today's match with shades of a man who knew all too well what was to lose. By the time he had found his feet he was a set down.

The deciding set tie-break is won by Berrettini. A narrow victory. The win of his career and what he has spent the whole year building up towards. This is the climax of all the young Italian's hard work and great results this season. Monfils is the nearly-man on this occasion.

Five sets. Signed, sealed, and delivered. One of the purest joys of tennis, in the past, the present, and surely the future. There is little denying the value of such matches, the nuances therein, and the glory and agony of how you exit the match tunnel.

Set

The first set in the Nadal v Schwartzman US Open quarter-final is a thing of beauty. As the whiplash tennis comes from one man's racket, then the other, and the score shifts in odd patterns, it becomes clear much rests on this opening set, now 5–4 to Nadal with Schwartzman serving to remain in it. Nadal had fired to a huge and relatively swift four-game lead, Schwartzman brought it back level with some lights-out tennis and now the set is teetering on the brink, both men with chances, the errors pressurised from each other's weapons. Nadal knows how sets like this are claimed, he maximises putting that experience and understanding into practice. He takes it 6–4 and goes on to win the match in three tight sets. Just what you want when two matches might remain.

DAY 11

The Canadian Decides the Outcome

Bianca Andreescu has forgotten how to lose, maybe didn't ever really know. Not as an adult, as the young woman she still is.

Her physical prowess, reminiscent of Serena or Rafa, is what sets her apart. Her youthful precociousness is another defining quality, but where other young players wear it as a badge of honour, an excuse for deficiencies, that ultimately brings them down, Andreescu uses it to her advantage, blindly and perhaps boldly stepping into unfamiliar terrain with the mindset that she can, of course, succeed. Why not? Why even contemplate the alternative outcomes. No question marks needed.

Occasionally, a player arrives who seems to blow everyone else out of the water. It doesn't matter who is ranked higher than, who is presently at number one, for every Bencic, Osaka, Sabalenka, Kasatkina, and so on, we are left talking about Andreescu this year because there is so much to talk about, and her game has set her for the very top. Once lodged there, on the world number one perch, toppling her might soon be a task nobody can handle. She looks like a queen in waiting.

She's 19. She's already won Indian Wells and the Rogers Cup this year. She's on the edge of the top 10. The sky is, literally, the limit, having started the year outside the top 150 female players. Add to that the fact that she missed most of the clay and grass court stages of the season, as the woman carves up the rankings like a much-craved Sunday roast.

The woman is a box office tennis sensation, an entertainer with huge shots, never-say-die attitude, brilliant on-court problem-solving skills. She gives bubbly and honest media interviews both on and off the court. She is also cultivating an almost pied piper following, which revels in seeing her in the limelight. She has a style of tennis, drama, and character that fans flock to. She gathers attention like flowers in a field. She appears to be an unstoppable train with a date with destiny.

You'd better believe one thing – Andreescu decides the outcome of a match. She's one of those few players whoseopponent, if she is on a hot streak, is inconsequential – she will (almost) certainly win her match. Even if she isn't swinging at her best, her mere presence, the physicality of her might undo her rival, as seen with Serena and other greats who impose themselves in multiple ways, all of them crucial and clinical. Andreescu will damage her opponent with brute force hitting that paints the lines, with unexpected delicacy, as well. She will be a one-woman stampede upon the hopes and dreams of others. She will believe she can keep her run going into the next match. Every single time.

Perhaps – if injury stays away – she will become indestructible.

DAY 12

Playing for History

Rafael Nadal has never been within one Grand Slam of Roger Federer's overall tally. The tennis purists will hate this. Whatever anyone says, this is what matters, this is where the legacies of these heroes will be secured. Nothing else means a jot. Not Nadal having the most Masters titles, not Djokovic and Federer having multiple titles of Nadal's elusive ATP Finals trophy. Not Nadal having Olympic singles gold while Roger and Novak don't. Not Djokovic having all nine Masters titles compared with the others who do not. People will refer to major triumphs. Plain and simple. Or is it?

These men go, playing for history, Novak Djokovic still trailing, also doing his best to catch up, to surpass. We know who has the most elegant game of the three, and who is the most elastic-limbed, and we know who has taken his game from his clearly favoured surface, redesigned it, and found a way past any obstacles to be considered in the argument, undeniably so, as the greatest player of all time.

If it comes down to slams, it's a close race. Not over yet. Closer by the year indeed.

Up All Night

The matches – the men's semi-finals – didn't go the distance, yet they lasted all night, regardless. Lengthy sets, some age-long sets, sets stretching their legs out into the night. Three sets, taking the time of much longer matches. A first set in each that passed the one-hour mark. Both matches lasted a total of around two and a half hours.

DAY 13

Ladies' Final

History repeating? Serena the Great, back in slam-winning form? The young (Bianca Andreescu) versus the legend. Two immense physical presences. One a teenage sensation of 2019. One a woman who needs no introduction, and since her comeback in the first half of 2018, has now amassed a total of four Grand Slam finals. Will this be the one she finally wins (thrice on the losing side of the net since Wimbledon 2018)? Will this Saturday night date see controversy? Will everyone be on their best behaviour? Many questions spring to mind given the two women who will share the stage on Saturday just after 4 pm New York time.

For Serena, it is slam 24 on the line to level with Margaret Court, with her sights then on number 25 to take the lead outright. No consideration is made of other players and, just perhaps, how tennis has moved on since she won the 2017 Australian Open. While no sensible tennis fan would bet against Serena equalling Court's record just yet, beating it might prove a step too far. If you are busy planning the expansion of your legacy, maybe it doesn't wait around and it seals its own door shut.

Today's final shows that Serena is no longer what she and many other people think she is – the ultimate female force in tennis. As a current player, she is in 'close but no cigar' territory. Her history is secure. Irrefutable. Her impact on women's tennis is astonishing. But she is far from the level of those she meets in slam finals. After four such cases against four different women (two at Wimbledon, two at the US Open – 2018 and 2019), it's inevitable that she should consider what all this means.

Bianca Andreescu played the match of the century – the quintessential fearless kid on the block who takes it to the past champion and rips her apart 6–3, 7–5.

Post-match, Serena details losing in finals as career 'downs'. Come on. Most players would love to reach finals and would consider them 'ups'. This is Serena. No normal rules apply. Is it just possible that she keeps ending up on the losing side because she hasn't shifted her goals realistically, aligned with the rest of the field?

Andreescu was unfazed. As good an example of that as you will see from a teenager. She tried and succeeded to block out the crowd, heavily in Serena's favour, who she was also playing against, and just to play her tennis. A remarkable skill at her age. If you have it, you have it. Andreescu has it in spades.

After Andreescu's impact on the early months of the season it was hard not to miss her through the European summer months. As she returned it felt like we had the chance to again witness the ascent of someone special. That is proven, capped, by her victory in New York, over the past Queen of Flushing Meadows.

Serena's choice of word by way of self-critique – 'inexcusable' – goes to show just what immense pressure she still has on herself to simply add to her tally of majors. Is she playing because she loves the sport? Can she see beyond those targets? She has been beaten, for the fourth time in her last four major finals, by players who simply looked to be enjoying their tennis more, without such a burden, easily able to put Serena to the sword, and that is probably where the key to these outcomes rests.

DAY 14

Men's Final

Whatever happens today, Daniil Medvedev is the real deal. Indubitably. Nobody really knows what to expect when a new face appears in a major final, as the Russian's does today. There is an odd atmosphere in Arthur Ashe stadium. Everyone is waiting to see how things proceed. Nadal a little uncertain at the off, Medvedev more like the experienced favourite. That switches, of course, and Nadal finds his feet, displaying his usual fight. There's a distinct tension. Rafael Nadal hits a blinding round-the-post shot, clipping the line on only the second point of the match. If it's anything to go by, we are in for a real humdinger.

Each player shows some flashes of brilliance. Nadal, seemingly more tentative than his young Russian opponent in his first Grand Slam final, knowing how much history is up for grabs today. Nadal with more to lose, surely.

The shot clock is Nadal's enemy. A nemesis ever in his way. Designed to slow his and others' progress (well, literally to speed them up and subsequently make them less likely to win) it hasn't quite had the impact on Nadal that some would have liked.

Games three and four of the opener are mutual breaks of service. Nadal doesn't seem himself today, appearing somewhat subdued.

Medvedev has shown so much character in the past month and a half, but even more since his errors of behaviour in the early rounds of this fortnight here in New York. He makes Rafa work for the title as seldom happens in the final match when not contested by members of the Big Three. Medvedev absolutely has NOT read the script for the final. Does he know about the Big Three and their stranglehold over the big trophies? He doesn't play as if he does. It's no classic – and no sign of being one – for the first two and a half sets. It heats up in its own way, launching an unexpected bomb halfway through the encounter. Perhaps the initial part of the match owes its imbalance to the pitting of a rookie finalist against one of the big guys with endless huge titles to his name. Maybe even the fact that Nadal could finally get to within just one slam of Roger's record is on people's minds.

Completely unexpectedly, it turns into a classic final when it goes to a fifth and final set. Medvedev levels at two sets all, after being two sets and a break down, and the match is then anybody's. A strange, unique, and memorable final that will come down to a one-set shoot-out in which Nadal has been below par and Medvedev has shown the world just what he is capable of. On one of the biggest stages, he has quietly announced himself. With the fanfare America loves, Medvedev has gone from pantomime villain to hero of the US Open 2019.

Nadal isn't at his best today. He isn't allowed to be, looking mentally rattled at certain stages throughout. He doesn't show it, but it comes off him, dripping like the ceaseless drops of sweat. Nadal looks fragile. Is he there for the taking? Medvedev somehow looks strong and vibrant, totally unfazed by his achievements in New York and any of this unravelling at the end of his incredible American hard-court season. It's phenomenal that he is still on his feet, punching above the weight anyone previously thought he could. This is a surprise. And yet not. At two sets to love the defeat could be smelled. New York, once again, treated to the very, very finest. In fact, it is the best men's final for several years thanks to 23-year-old Daniil Medvedev fighting to the end, just as his Spanish opponent always does.

If at first it seems anticlimactic, it will come to life, it will stand tall, it will soon become known as a phenomenal final. Yesterday, Andreescu gave the people what they didn't know they wanted, longing for Serena's twenty-fourth as they had been, blind to Andreescu's promise and magnificence. They had witnessed the passing of the baton, the genuine arrival of someone remarkably special, and a match of odd intrigue and beauty. And Daniil Medvedev had done the same. Announced himself and shown exactly what he could do and what made him the most likely –

after all the names touted along the way – to break the Big Three for good, to shatter it into pieces.

From start to finish, this is an unusual and memorable affair, an outlier, a strange but talented child. The old(er) and the young. The experienced and the fearless. The Russian, the Spaniard. The one competing for history versus the one after a first major and a small etching on the board of the tournament's present, and therefore past and future.

The atmosphere in set five is literally off the chart. As the noise dies, as the men strike each clinical wound upon the other, piercing armour, a surge, paused, and the other presses on. And Nadal strikes a blow. Having almost gone 2–0 down, he lands the punch to hopefully do the damage. He breaks, much against the grain, unbelievably, in set five and leads 3–2. He will serve next. If he holds his next three service games – and it seems a big ask right now – he will win the US Open for his fourth time and make it Grand Slam number 19. He does indeed seal a huge win. Had Medvedev found a way to win it would surely have been one of the greatest comebacks in the history of tennis. He had several break points on Nadal's serve for a 2-0 lead in the final set. Had Nadal not saved those – had he had a moment's dip in concentration, we may be discussing a wholly different story. As it was, and for the umpteenth time, Nadal found a way through the maze. A Russian maze of distinction. And what a way to conquer. Number 19 in the pocket.

And if people do not respect Daniil Medvedev by now then they never will. The part he has played has been immense, but this slice of history is destined for Nadal. Rafa found a way to one of the key wins of his entire career in a strange and thrilling final. Medvedev, take a bow. Progress from the young guns? You bet! Rafael Nadal went truly beyond himself to win it 7–5, 6–3, 5–7, 4–6, 6–4 though.

4 OCTOBER 2019

Murray Comeback Gathers Speed

I

Over the course of 2019, Matteo Berrettini has proven himself as a top 20 player (pushing the top 10 even) who, on his day, is very difficult to beat with his brutal flowing baseline tennis, as he thumps scud missiles from all over the court.

Being drawn against said Italian – the number eight seed – in round one of this China Open is exactly the type of challenge that Andy Murray would relish, just the test he's looking at getting his teeth into as he looks to end the season strongly. It's a comeback with eyes trained on it, with optimism coming from multiple quarters.

It's a match of peaks and troughs until Murray does indeed bag a huge win over one of the form players of the year. After two tie-breaks, the match is decided in favour of Andy Murray. Hope renewed, the future looking brighter for Murray and his followers, and it's been a while since it felt even remotely that way.

II

Look out, 2020, Andy Murray is back! Today he played in the China Open quarter-final today against Dominic Thiem. Thiem is a regular top 10 fixture these days, ranked as high as four in the past. Forget the loss, it can hardly come as a surprise, focus on the manner, on the fight coming from the Scot and his racket, happily hand in hand again on a professional tennis stage. Ponder the journey to get back to here, post-hip operation, and compete at this level again – 2020 could have some real magic in store for Murray fans as he hopes to ride the building wave into the new season. His wins this week and some of his work against Thiem shows a man in the ascendency once more. The body now doing as it's requested; these matches will stand him in good stead.

III

Swings and roundabouts in the European Open final as Andy Murray sends out a warning shot to everybody of his presence a little over two weeks after his loss to Dominic Thiem in China. Murray wins against Stanislas Wawrinka 3–6, 6–4, 6–4. The Scot is a phenomenal athlete and ambassador for tennis, a never-say-die attitude almost unrivalled. What a comeback. I for one cannot wait to see more.

Federer and Zverev Serve Up a Feast

Five match points was not enough to see Sascha Zverev over the line for a 2–0 win over Roger Federer as the Swiss used the crowd, his magic book, and his entire catalogue of skill, savvy, and experience to bank the second set and take it to a decider in the pair's seventh encounter, this time in the Shanghai Masters quarter-final.

Roger's tantrum in set three takes something away from an amazing match, more than threatening to ruin what had been becoming a delectable feast. And, as with the end of year ATP Finals last year, Federer and (some of) his (let's face it) somewhat crazy fans are spoiling another match with Zverev.

It feels as much that it is Federer here who undoes himself as it is Zverev, who, make no mistake, has been wonderful once more today, playing his way back into some cracking form. The Federer hurdle is a complicated one, and Zverev has coped incredibly well on more than one occasion. For, whoever wins today will lead the pair's head-to-head by four match wins to three.

It's beautiful that Zverev holds on for the win, against the crowd, possibly the most naturally gifted player ever, and the distractions of Federer's blatant moaning.

Zverev roars with joy as he crosses the finishing line in glory and it's his first win over a top 10 player all year, thoroughly deserved, and the mark of a man finding some incredible tennis in the late stages of the season after struggling on and off the court all year long.

So, yes, set three was odd, an anticlimax of unusual proportions. Federer got a point penalty for hitting a ball out of the court once too often. It could have come sooner. Rules are rules. A slightly bitter taste remains on what should have been a wonderful occasion with a win for Zverev that signals a return to his best.

Impenetrable Medvedev

Stefanos Tsitsipas, fresh from beating Novak Djokovic well in three sets the day before, proved no match for Daniil Medvedev – who continues in the form of his young life – today. Another straight-sets win, and he now hasn't lost a set since that US Open final with Rafael Nadal last month. It's no fluke, he looks destined for the top of the tree, and Tsitsipas, at the end of the day, is 5–0 down in the pair's head-to-head, making it a match-up that the Greek simply cannot work out.

Daniil Medvedev looks impenetrable, unplayable, impossible to get much from, other than a share of serves it's hard to do much with and a handshake at the end of the encounter. Nadal only just pipped him in New York and, since then, if anything, the Russian has gone from strength to strength. He's now into his sixth final from his last six events, has won the most matches this year on the ATP tour, and looks like the clear favourite for a second Masters title (here in Shanghai), which he does indeed go on to win (beating Zverev in a rather one-sided final). By the end of the week, it's nine wins in a row – 18 sets on the trot. A man on fire on the tennis court.

Here's Coco!

Cori Gauff had already arrived, announcing herself by beating one of her heroines, Venus Williams, at this year's Wimbledon. Such a stage for defeating someone you admire is one hell of a way to launch a career, and it took her name to the global tennis public. 'Coco' was the nickname on everyone's lips, ringing out loud as everyone immediately fell in love with the teenager.

On the cusp of a huge ranking breakthrough, she has reached the final in Linz, Austria, thereby entering the world's top hundred and signalling an exciting 2020 ahead.

In the final today, who'd be surprised if the sufficiently older 22-year-old Jeļena Ostapenko proved no match. Ostapenko has been in poor form for a year or two now since her own breakthrough year of 2017.

However, Gauff claims the first set, is pegged back in the second, and storms to glory to take it in the decider. Ostapenko had a chance for a first title in ages and was schooled by a teenager. She was once issuing such lessons. This day, however, is about a remarkable new talent. Cori Gauff is going to be very special indeed. The new decade about to open its gates will surely see her at the top of women's tennis. Let's hope she manages to retain her warmth and intelligence. The game needs such gentle, thoughtful, and inspirational personalities.

Fearless Schwartzman Doesn't Quite Break Thiem's Home Crowd's Hearts

Over one set, Diego Schwartzman can beat practically anyone. As we've seen against Nadal and other players and here again today against home favourite, Dominic Thiem. The Argentine plays a brand of tennis undaunted by big names, styles, and reputations.

His hard-hitting approach and ability to move opponents around and make them thoroughly uncomfortable has lifted him to some lofty heights in the world of tennis, lodged inside the world's top 20, as he is.

However, Thiem finally wins (3–6, 6–4, 6–3) the much sought-after Vienna Open title (in his homeland) that he had been dreaming about since childhood. That must be one hell of a feeling. You cannot help but feel Thiem needs to push on, realise that potential we have witnessed, especially on clay, and find his way to a few Grand Slam titles. He's stuck, age-wise, between the greats and the new kids on the block. The window will, perhaps, not last forever. On his day, he's a glorious sight to behold, hitting that one-handed backhand and burying shots, winners flowing, as if they were secrets that needed hiding from view.

The Colour Is Purple

The WTA Finals have moved on from Singapore to Shenzhen, and the court is a pink, punky purple, brighter and not as delicate as the pink of Petra Kvitová's dress in the first match of this year's ladies' showpiece event. The court is piercing as is some of the tennis. It's another flamboyant tennis event in the modern sphere: loud, eye-catching, busy, just like a teenager demanding to be seen and heard.

This year's two Australian Open finalists – Petra Kvitová and Naomi Osaka – serve up a close and fascinating opener to the WTA Finals, which are a prize for the eight women present, a culmination of all the hard work over the course of the year.

Naomi Osaka wins a tight first set with a snatched tie-break, unleashing her best and most clinical tennis when the moment demanded it. Petra breaks several times in set two, the decisive one handing her the set 6–4.

Horns are locked. A final set commences. The ladies have taken no time whatsoever to warm up to this tournament. Osaka, once again, has Kvitová's number and wins 7–6, 4–6, 6–4.

Halep v Andreescu

Today's match surely indicates things to come in 2020.

The tables turned in this match, the pendulum swung back and forth, and the time ticked on, the crowd becoming ever more invested in this early WTA Finals classic. The push and the pull.

With Simona Halep a break down in the final set. At 1–2, she bursts back to break and hold serve and break again, thereby giving herself a 4–2 lead. That, however, as has been the way of things during this encounter, is not that, and she is routinely broken straight back for 4–3. Andreescu will serve to level this crazy match once more that could end up in the purse of either woman.

Nobody can be remotely surprised when Halep comes back, ever the counterpuncher, preferring to attack and break the serve of others than to serve herself. She does punch holes in Andreescu, breaking once more, making it 5–3 and giving herself the chance to serve it out if she can hold serve this time. It is soon 30–0 and Halep is closing in on another impressive win. 40–0. She serves it out to love. 3–6, 7–6, 6–3.

I reckon this pair will play again come the final on Sunday.*

This prediction would turn out to be wholly inaccurate, with neither woman reaching the final. It also reminds me very well why I tend to refrain from making predictions.

THE CLOSE OF THE DECADE

NOVEMBER 2019

The Bagel Set

The Simona Halep Enigma. There's your subtitle for this text. She's up, she's down, nobody knows which version of the diminutive Romanian will turn up. The frustrating task of the returned coach Darren Cahill is there for all to see. It's the WTA Finals and Halep has just been handed a bagel by Karolína Plíšková.

Cahill comes on to the court post-bagel set for some tinkering. Adjustments are made. Let's try again …

Set one is not the match. Reset. Go again, wake up, and … Boom! Early break and she's on the board. 2–0 Halep. Broken back. 2–2. Halep breaks again and holds. 4–2, another break. 5–2. The first set forgotten. The second set soon done and dusted when Halep claims it 6–2. Plíšková is also known for capitulation episodes.

Sets two and three are simply a story of service breaks. Plíšková, with by far the most potent serve of the two, fails to retain it when needed and Halep freely gives hers up all too often. With Plíšková 5–2 up, the end appears in sight. The Halep serve, frail again, offers three chances for the Czech to take the match and head into tomorrow's semis. Halep clings on. 3–5. Plíšková is again broken, and it reeks of one of those matches nobody knows how to win. 4–5 Halep trails. We've been here and seen this before. Typical Halep. And, yes, Plíšková too. A frustrating pair to watch at times, let alone sit in the camp of. Halep serves to level in the decider, having led 2–0 and then lost five games in a row. Halep faces a break point though, and Plíšková seals the win and semi-final berth.

Against other players, Plíšková might not have got out of that one alive. Halep, along with the returned maestro Cahill may well have to get back to the drawing board and make a ferocious plan for 2020. On today's showing, further grafting is required. The chasing pack is only getting bigger, stronger, and better.

Later, Tsitsipas narrowly avoids a first-set bagel by Novak Djokovic in the men's Paris Masters quarter-finals, eventually claiming his third and final service game of the set before Djokovic polishes off the near immaculate set 6–1. 0–40 had become deuce and converted into a game on the board for the frustrated young Greek. Tsitsipas is getting obliterated here though. How do you change that? Well, sometimes you can't, and while this match didn't deliver a bagel set, the outcome of 6–1, 6–2 in favour of Djokovic will certainly not feel great to the Greek man on the losing end of it.

Final Final

The women's season came to its conclusion today with the season ending, show-stopping WTA Finals final. It pitted the defending champion Elina Svitolina against the world number one Ashleigh Barty, each lady proving themselves more than able over the last week, and more impressively the year, of coming back from a set down.

Barty's cool tennis and attitude had just edged the first set, with the second being responsible for traded blows via breaks of serve coming thick and fast. Barty broke to get her nose in front and then got broken instead of going within one game of the title. Then another close Svitolina service game ensued, and the Ukrainian failed to cling on to level at 4–4, instead Barty is one game away at 5–3. Barty serves it out to love. Happy days! There will be no third set for these women today, no comeback.

It's a clear gulf between the finalists, and Barty tops off her year as the undoubted world number one.

A match is often won by the player who just had a little – or a lot – more to get over the line, and when looking at the season preceding this event and match, you can't argue that a world number one and Roland Garros champion isn't a fitting first-time winner of the WTA Finals title. Barty will not be easy to shift from her pedestal in 2020.

The Birth of the Baby-Faced Assassin

ATP NextGen Final – Alex de Minaur v Jannik Sinner

Just as the year started with the shape of kids (Canadian ones) exploding out of the blocks to essentially define the year as something different from its predecessors, it ends with a youngster taking down everyone in sight.

The names bring shades of darkness to the final of the third instalment of the ATP NextGen Finals – Demon (de Minaur's nickname) and Sinner (a new Italian maverick on the scene). Sinner is confident, aggressive, and lost in his game. Sinner plays a neat, powerful game, much as de Minaur does. The young Italian looks oblivious to the stage, the occasion, what is on the line.

Sinner, with some explosive returns, breaks de Minaur serving to stay in the opener and it's a lovely lead, in his homeland (the event based in Milan, Italy), and more than enough to get de Minaur contemplating what a large task he might have here today to avoid a second consecutive year with the NextGen runners-up trophy.

Sinner is phenomenally calm and clued in, somehow the image of tranquillity, more so than de Minaur, who had looked that way himself all week. A chat with his coach post-set one reveals de Minaur to be rather irked, game face slipping.

If ranking and experience mean anything, the Australian would win the match. If form and the confidence of youth were to have their say, which they currently are doing, Sinner may well prove impossible to beat tonight. He presently leads de Minaur by 4–2, 2–0. (The NextGen is unique with sets played to four rather than the standard six.)

This kind of fearless Sinner approach is what the Grand Slams need from the youngsters. His defence is total attack and, when facing break points, he unleashes a lethal serve and groundstroke combination onto the court and averts the danger. It is at times volcanic. He takes the second set to lead by two sets to love and be in a position that perhaps few would have predicted.

Sinner feels no sympathy and will feel no remorse for so mercilessly punishing a world top-20 player in de Minaur, whom he has, on this occasion, shown up on the big stage. For de Minaur, it will be a loss that might prove hard to shake as he ponders how to move further up the rankings. Let us hope he quickly bounces back as Sinner nails his opponent's coffin lid shut. De Minaur shows poor body language as it comes to its end and appears negative when talking to his coach. Staying positive regardless is a crucial element of a successful player. You must simply believe in your game, whatever your opponent is doing. It's unusual that de Minaur has taken it so badly, not found any solutions to the barrage from Sinner's racket, and became despondent quite so early in today's encounter. After losing the first set, his coach said, 'don't give up!' as if he could foresee that happening.

Such a mature performance from Sinner, whose serve afforded him a level of security that few players can bring themselves. Brilliant scenes as Sinner takes it in three straight short sets. Sinner was the lowest ranked player in the event this week (at 93 in the world), and seeded eighth for the week, but he is the first native champion in Milan. He comprehensively outplayed his older and more experienced opponent, introducing himself, at only 18 years of age to the global tennis crowd. This was, indeed, the birth of the baby-faced assassin from Italy.

Blockbuster

Day five of the ATP Finals sees the much-eyed Björn Borg group clash between its two most well-known and successful men, Roger Federer, and Novak Djokovic – the one you couldn't make up if you tried, a blockbuster, make no mistake.

In something of a surprise in the previous two days of play of the round-robin phase, both men had succumbed to the switched-on power and brilliance of Dominic Thiem (as well as both having beaten ATP Finals first-timer Matteo Berrettini), meaning, essentially, that whoever won this would go into the semi-finals on Saturday. In the other group (Andre Agassi), the permutations meant it was a little less clear heading into the final day of group matches the next day.

Here we are though. The box office thriller of the group stage, considering the past matches of the pair and their last, yes, whisper it, encounter, at Wimbledon 2019 in THAT epic and brain-blistering final. These are two men who have shared a 48-match rivalry, with Djokovic leading the head-to-head 26–22. It's match number 49 and it has 'special' written all over it, people salivating in expectant hope for something rekindling the mad magic of that 13–12 final set at Wimbledon some months ago. The loss today will end the season with a whimper, somewhat against expectations.

Federer is almost the only player on earth who can rattle Djokovic – especially as the Swiss has ANY given crowd in his pocket, firmly on his side – and that shows when Djokovic is soon at 0–40 on his serve; Federer forcing his opponent's errors as the tightness becomes apparent. It's one of Roger's greatest magic tricks. It isn't just tennis now, it's a spell that nobody has ever been able to conduct on a tennis court, affecting the mental state of all who come up against him. Federer takes the first break point and is 2–1 up.

Federer hits the ball so early, so effortlessly, it's like he's sweeping up, leaving any mess for dead, a trail of nothing but his balletic feet gliding. Djokovic just can't reach his usual game, isn't allowed. It's startling to watch. That unbreakable aura is absent from the Serb's game and facing the pro-Roger crowd affects Novak greatly. You get the feeling it's the ultimate stuff of nightmares for him.

It somehow doesn't feel like a fair contest. Roger is sublime, brutal, an executioner with no mercy. Whether it's the extreme crowd support or Federer's swift ease at casting aside Djokovic's usual weapons, or perhaps the weight of what is on the line (if Djokovic loses here, he cannot regain the world number one ranking for the year end); it barely feels like there are two men involved in the match. It's eerie, painful, exquisite.

Federer maintains his brilliant serving routine and keeps holding to see the early break over the line to its desired conclusion and captures the set 6–4. In set two, it's more of the same, a relentless bombardment upon Djokovic. The treatment Djokovic normally directs towards others. It all looks so easy for the Swiss tonight; once again, Djokovic imploding, Djokovic unable to contend with the magician and his loyal army of vocal supporters (Djokovic would love to get such support though it will now never be more than a lost dream). You can turn away from the action and know who wins every point based purely on the pro-Roger cacophony or the near-silent whisper when Djokovic prevails.

The question remains whether Federer can continue to serve at this level for the entirety of the match, as Djokovic would be ready to pounce. When Federer finds this groove in a match though, he rarely loses it.

At 1–2, Djokovic gets his first break point of the match at 30–40 on the Federer serve. Federer comes up with a remarkable point, pushing Djokovic into both corners of the court before putting away a simple volley. Danger averted. Federer saves and then gets what might prove to be the crucial break of the Djokovic serve to lead 3–2.

Nadal fans everywhere are hoping Roger finishes what he has so beautifully built here (if he does, Rafa will retain the year-end number one spot). He has the Serb right where he wants him. Federer serves out to 30 and takes a 4–2 lead, Djokovic's year is set to end on a low note. It's soon 5–3 to Federer and it's an assured performance, a warning shot to the others, and the kind that indicates he is *nowhere near* retirement.

This level is mind boggling. For any player. Let alone one of 38 years of age. He does make it hard not to focus on his age a little. It simply doesn't follow the laws of logic. He has totally outplayed the world number two, a man six years younger and often seen as an invincible force. It's hard to believe, based on this, that the Swiss lost their previous encounter in such devastating fashion in that heart-breaking Wimbledon final.

Federer defeats Djokovic in straight sets, rather easily, to be frank. It's Federer's first win over his Serbian nemesis since 2015. That will feel remarkably good and signal an exciting year ahead, should they meet again.

Last Orders

With the Big Three present at the start of the week, who would've predicted today's final being between ATP Finals first-timer 21-year-old Stefanos Tsitsipas and 26-year-old Dominic Thiem, in the final showpiece match for his first time too, meaning another new champion would be crowned and he would be the fifth different winner in as many years?

The bell has been rung for the last orders and there'll be one more match at the O2 and in the world of men's tennis this year. The women have already swanned off for a well-earned rest and the men – bar those in the imminent Davis Cup final – have now reached the last of the magic for another decade.

Will it provide a fitting finale? Tsitsipas serves first. An impressive opening is pocketed in four straight points by the Greek. Then it is Thiem's turn. Anything you can do … He also wins his first service game of the final to love. And Tsitsipas holds to 30. The new faces at this stage give fans a chance to pick their allegiance, all over again, without the legendary granddaddies of the sport overseeing everything as they have in recent years. Thiem has been around a while now but is improving year on year. Tsitsipas plays tennis in a more Federer-esque mould and ignites the emotions of crowds more readily. Both men the worthy of backing, especially based on their performances this week. It's soon 3–2 to the Greek. A couple of hairy moments in the last games are bypassed and serve is held once more by Thiem to make it 3–3.

Thiem then gets to 30–40 for a look at a first break point. He had faced and saved one himself earlier and now Tsitsipas does the same. Deuce. Thiem fashions another break point as Tsitsipas's groundstrokes fail. The point is replayed owing to a mistaken call of 'out'. Tsitsipas wins the replayed point. Deuce. And two points later he has once more held his serve. 4–3.

As the set advances the tension rises, the players taut and on the edge, surviving on serve, but only just. And finally, it ends with a tie-break, Thiem scraping his way into it.

The immediate mini break goes the way of Thiem. 1–0. Big hitting takes him to 2–0. Two crucial holds and the tie-break is looking very one-sided at 3–0. It's soon 5–3 to Thiem. Is Tsitsipas clawing his way back into it? 5–4. Two Thiem serves to come. Mini break retrieved. 5–5. 6–6. Neither man cracking now. Second change of ends of the breaker. Tsitsipas with a messy backhand that goes long. 7–6. The set is on Thiem's racket now. And he serves hard and it's too much for Tsitsipas. Thiem has a one-set lead.

The start of the second set sees the first break of the match as Tsitsipas breaks Thiem to 15 and seizes the early advantage. The Greek is soon 2–0 up. Thiem is then broken again to trail 0–3 and the set looks done. A couple of holds, and 4–1 in favour of Tsitsipas edges the set closer to its rather uneven ending, nothing like its predecessor. 5–2. And in the blink of an eye, it's over. 6–2 to Stefanos.

A final set ensues. The battle resumes. Thiem squeezes through his service game and it's 1–0. Soon after, Thiem buckles under the pressure when facing two break points. He saves the first and hits a backhand into the net on the second. A long way back now. Thiem 1–2 down. Tsitsipas bottles another easy service hold. 3–1. Thiem then holds to 30, but perhaps the damage has been done. He hasn't broken his opponent's serve all evening.

But Thiem does come back at Tsitsipas. He starts to find what he hasn't in the last set and a half and, seeking to bring back parity to the final set, he gets to 15–30 on his rival's serve. Tsitsipas looking a little tight suddenly. 15–40. Two break points, and now would be the perfect moment to get his first break of the Tsitsipas serve in the entire match. He goes long with the first, with only himself to blame. He looks mad now. But then a Tsitsipas error hands the break to Thiem. 3–3. All square again. It has indeed turned into a blinding last match of the year, season, and decade. From out of nowhere, Thiem has stormed back, giving his opponent nothing again. He serves to love with some brutal hitting and he leads 4–3. In fact, he leads in a set for the first time since winning the opening set. Tsitsipas emerges from a tight service game to hold and it's 4–4. It's a real a tug of war between the two men as the crowd wills the pair on. Thiem, in the ascendency again, holds serve, making it 5–4 and putting the pressure greatly back on Tsitsipas's shoulders. Tsitsipas holds in 67 seconds and puts Thiem back into bat. 5–5. A final-set tie-break is looming. Thiem serves his way there. It's just up to Tsitsipas to join him there or fall.

And ... Tsitsipas serves. He goes just wide with a groundstroke. 0–15. Thiem goes long. Mistakes shooting off both rackets now. 15–15. Tsitsipas in at the net and survives a Thiem lob by burying a smash off it. 30–15. 40–15. A point away from a deciding tie-break. Thiem with a huge forehand cross court and it's 40–30. Life in this game yet. Thiem goes long though, a flame snuffed out. Tsitsipas strangling the service game and meeting Thiem in a final-set tie-break. This is how the year ends, this is how the curtain falls.

Thiem to open it. Big serve. Return goes long. Thiem 1–0. Thiem also hits a shot long and it's 1–1. Tsitsipas gets the party started by holding again. He takes the lead at 2–1. Thiem then crumbles and gives both service points away. 4–1 to the younger of the two men, Tsitsipas. Rock solid then from Thiem to draw the error from the other side of the net. 4–2 at the change of ends. Thiem with unparalleled aggression and he gets the double mini break back. 4–3 down but Thiem serving next. Insane backhand from Thiem to get to 4–4. Explosive. Absolutely explosive. Then, Thiem makes a mistake and is down again. 5–4 to Tsitsipas with two Greek serves to come. A long rally, but ultimately Thiem messes it up. 6–4. Match points to the youngster. The big-money serve just misses. Tsitsipas then slams the door shut and wins the biggest title of his career so far. Only Nadal beat him all week. What a match, Tsitsipas winning the event on his debut in the ATP Finals.

The Davis Cup Final 2019

Madrid was a happy city as its Davis Cup team took its place in the final against Canada. Rafael Nadal and co. had been firing on all cylinders and, bar the news that Roberto Bautista Agut lost his father mid-week, it's been a brilliant run for the Spanish in front of a pumped home crowd this week in the new-look Davis Cup. With the changed format and the imminently rolled-out international team competition the ATP Cup – also on the men's side – you could argue that tennis is going to a new place altogether.

The final today starts with Bautista Agut himself – who hasn't played since the early part of the week – up against wunderkind Félix Auger-Aliassime. With plenty of Canadian flags, it's still obvious whose backyard this is being played in.

Both men have a 50–50 Davis Cup record. The difference is Bautista Agut has 14 matches split down the middle and Mr Auger-Aliassime only has two (one win and one loss earlier this week in his first year appearing in the tournament).

The chants of 'Roberto!' after his straight-sets victory are surely music to his ears, a fitting epitaph to his rocky week. For a man who has really gone through the mill in recent years. he continues, nevertheless, to go from strength to strength on a tennis court, still improving with the years.

Nadal, with 28 wins and one loss in Davis Cup singles, has the best record in the competition ever. It's business as usual in set one of the second match, with Nadal and Shapovalov level for a while, until Nadal pulls out into the lead and doesn't look back. With the capture of the opening set, for him, for Spain, it's just a set away from a first Davis Cup title since 2011 for the Spanish.

At 4–4, 30–30 in the second set – with Nadal's Spain a set to the good already – Nadal hits a passing shot, so ferocious and so perfect it needs repeat plays to believe, to get to break point. Shapovalov quickly wipes out the chance and leads 5–4, hoping for the tie-break lottery to see if he can keep the final alive.

It's been Nadal's year, and this is the cherry on the cake, and Spain will be swollen with pride after a fierce and impressive win on home soil. At the end, you cannot help but feel Roberto Bautista Agut is the king of the day, the week, and even his homeland on this occasion. As Nadal closes in on victory, the cameraman shows Bautista Agut. Perhaps it's normal to wonder what is going through his head so soon after such a sad personal loss, but he has performed like a true professional and he deserves every inch of limelight and every accolade bestowed upon him. I, personally, hope Bautista Agut is somehow able to savour the fruits of this team triumph – with Nadal winning in two straight sets – despite his terribly tough week. Character is built and shown over time. You cannot announce it. It's these moments in which the real heart and beauty of women and men emerges. Spain the perfect winners of the brand-new Davis Cup.

6 AN ANNOUNCEMENT
DECEMBER 2019

Wozniacki Calls Time

Many factors can contribute to a player calling time on their career. On the women's side there are additional considerations that are unavoidable at some point. Caroline Wozniacki – at 29 years of age, and with one Grand Slam title in her bank and a highest ranking of world number one – has accomplished what she set out to, experienced some health issues in more recent years, seen the youngsters coming up from behind, and has decided enough is enough and the desire to have a family has a pull that cannot be left on hold.

Here is a player who leaves a great impression on the last decade or so. There have been quite a few Grand Slam winners in that period, and some have won more, not all reaching the pinnacle of women's tennis as Wozniacki has. Regarding a legacy, Wozniacki has designed herself as an incredibly tough competitor more than capable of unexpected comebacks. Wozniacki has won many titles – 30 – and truly left her mark by winning the 2018 Australian Open and the WTA Finals in 2017 as well.

Wozniacki has been a constant hurdle to others over the past decade, she takes a great well of on-court memories, some at the world's finest events, and will move into the next phase of her life with very few regrets. The last few weeks of her career, until she retires in Melbourne (at the Australian Open, the site of her greatest triumph), could well see her swinging like there's nothing left to do, or say, and that could make her even more dangerous.

7 DOWN UNDER
JANUARY 2020

An Australian Cauldron

Roberto Bautista Agut is the picture of cool as he puts Nick Kyrgios to the sword in their ATP Cup match in the semi-final tie between Spain and Australia (in the land down under). More focused, clinical, mature, and hungry than his opponent, Bautista Agut is not to be messed with.

As Bautista Agut made Kyrgios look average (which, let's face it, maybe, just maybe, he is), the Spaniard's rock-solid mentality and performance to match is what has undone the Aussie enigma/madman/talent/_____ (insert your own word here).

Next up, Rafael Nadal steps into the Australian cauldron to take on Alex de Minaur. The young Australian has really started to impose himself upon the top end of the men's game in recent times (let's forget his disappointing runner-up spot in the NextGen final only two months ago) and is a threat, especially on a hard court in his own backyard.

De Minaur is all over Nadal in set one, a caged beast released. Remind you of anyone? The question in such cases is always whether it can be sustained or not. While de Minaur wins the opener – the first set in three matches against Nadal that he has ever won – by the halfway point in set two (3–3) he looks tired and less pumped, sweaty, and a little more drawn, rather just hanging with Nadal now. He's continuing to play solid tennis, but it feels like Nadal might soon pounce.

The answer, that I guess is obvious, is that de Minaur cannot keep up with Rafa, narrowly losing set two and being broken early in the final set for Nadal to take charge 2–0 and grind him down. Nadal does finish him off then, and thereby Spain wins the tie and heads into the final with Serbia (which Serbia will win 2–1, led by Nenad Zimonjić).

The Moutet Landing

Corentin Moutet, the 20-year-old Frenchman and world number 80, is making waves over in Doha. He has sealed his spot in the final of the Qatar Open and will find the Russian block that is Andrey Rublev there.

The young Frenchman does go on to lose to the ever-ascending Rublev, but it's certainly a week that underlines Moutet's own credentials early in the year. The plethora of new young talent is undeniable, and it is now a question of how many faces and how soon those folks will push up through to the higher echelons of the sport. Just as we are talking about one or two handfuls of brilliant new talent, the next ones, even younger, start to make their presence known and push their way through.

Rublev is on fire right now, so there's no shame in losing to a man in such form, but remember the name 'Moutet', as it's certainly only the beginning of what he is capable of.

Serena Turns It on in Auckland

A blistering start to 2020 is just what the doctor ordered for Serena Williams. Matches under the belt, a definite confidence in the face of once more going for that elusive twenty-fourth Grand Slam record-equalling title, and the rhythm that many would insist had been missing in previous Grand Slam attempts over the past two years.

Winning the title in Auckland – and let us not forget that it is the legend's first title of any kind in almost three years (since she won the 2017 Australian Open) – was perfectly timed to establish Serena as this year's favourite going into Melbourne's major, and to give her the self-belief that perhaps was not quite there since childbirth (whatever might have been said).

A New Decade

Nature will out, as much as Roger Federer, Serena Williams, Rafael Nadal, and Novak Djokovic are defiant in the face of the ageing process, they are extremely unlikely to be the names people have on their lips when considering the players of this new decade, come its ending.

While the impact of those four players is unfathomable in the grand context of tennis and what had come before their careers, they will all meet their professional-tennis-playing-career makers in the coming years.

Who will be the ones whose names are whispered, nay, shouted from the rooftops in celebration of consistent brilliance? Well, the beauty of sport is that nothing can be certain and even less when predicting 40 Grand Slams' worth of action across a decade entire, and who might just emerge the face(s) of that period in both the men's and women's games. Will it be someone we already know well – such as Andreescu, Tsitsipas, Bencic, and Auger-Aliassime – or someone yet to crash onto the scene under the public gaze? You might well have 15-year-old Cori Gauff on the mind when considering imminent future greatness.

8 AUSTRALIAN OPEN 2020

DAY 3

Roberto Bautista Agut Keeps Up 2020 Form

While he isn't having everything his own way, dropping the opening set in his second-round match with Michael Mmoh today, Roberto Bautista Agut is one hell of a force to be reckoned with right now. On the back of the finest year of his career and fuelled by loss, Bautista Agut started the year winning all six of his singles matches at the ATP Cup. With his second win here in Melbourne, he is getting on a run that makes him a dangerous opponent for anyone. Sitting in the same half of the draw as Novak Djokovic and Swiss maestro Roger Federer (potential quarter and semi matches respectively), it's not going to be an easy task to go deep. Nevertheless, it's unlikely anyone will want to face the Spaniard in such brutally wonderful form.

Roberto Bautista Agut missed his maiden appearance at the O2 last season by losing one final match that, had he won, would have seen him qualify. If he can be as consistent this year, even with the greats and brilliant youngsters out there, who would bet against him making it to the London event that hosts the best eight men of the year this time around.

Hurkacz Tumbles Tamely Out

A double fault to let the first set go when serving at 4–5 will hopefully prove the catalyst for Hubert Hurkacz to get his head down. He's played some good tennis of late – no better way forwards than to convert that to the biggest stages and realise some new wins – and pushed his way into the seedings at the Australian Open and thereby given himself a chance in the early rounds in Melbourne.

That he is facing Australian John Millman in front of a baying crowd makes life a little harder. Hurkacz never quite manages to join the occasion and excel, in the end succumbing to a rather feeble straight-sets defeat 6–4, 7–5, 6–3. While Millman is by no means a pushover, you cannot help but feel players like Hurkacz and Tiafoe (first round loss to Medvedev) need to start finding a way to overcome some of the higher-ranked and more-experienced players if they are to join them in the top 20 of the game.

DAY 5

Gauff v Osaka

It's hard to fathom a 15-year-old girl being box office tennis, but there's no denying the pull and impact of young Cori 'Coco' Gauff. She has more than just a chance of being something great. At such a tender age, to be this good is noteworthy.

When Gauff breaks and then serves out the opening set against defending champion Naomi Osaka it looks like an enormous moment in women's tennis is about to take place, even a seminal moment that makes us all ask, 'Where were you when …?'

Gauff's calm demeanour, her total ability to use the crazy environment inside the arena and under the lights to her favour, and her brilliant tennis make her already lethal to any other player out there. Forget age. It doesn't matter much here.

Osaka simply cannot cope, having to admire Gauff along with the rest of us. She can't be 15. FIFTEEN!!! It's surreal.

Gauff is broken back early in set two after an initial break to the younger of the two. And at 3–3, Gauff breaks Osaka again for 4–3 and serves next. She holds easily and is a game from an early decade-defining win.

The ease with which Gauff serves it out 6–3, 6–4 is remarkable. A star was already born. This is a supernova. This is not normal.

Gauff seems surprised. After the match in the on-court interview, Gauff states that just two years earlier she lost in the first round of the juniors' event. Today's match is a major upset, and yet not. The apple cart of women's tennis has been rather disturbed today.

Marathon Man

On paper, this match between Marin Čilić (past runner-up) and Roberto Bautista Agut (in lethal form of late) looked like the highlight of the third round. On the Melbourne Arena court, it turns into the men's match of the tournament so far, later today to be outshone by the Federer v Millman match.

Wired and dialled in is the best way to sum up today's version of Marin Čilić. His stock has fallen over the past year or so as he has struggled with form, and he is ranked outside the automatic seeding spots (39 in the world at present), meaning very much that Bautista Agut was the favourite beforehand. It doesn't matter that Bautista Agut is in the form of his life, all that counts is that Čilić hits a groove and becomes unstoppable as we have all seen him do before (even claiming a major title at the US Open in 2014).

After losing the first set on a tie-break, Čilić presses on with some brutal hitting, pushing Bautista Agut to his limit and shattering him in the process. Čilić breaks at the end of set two and serves it out.

He then continues that streak and ferociously brings down the axe on the Spaniard handing him a third-set bagel. He then breaks in set four to close in on the finishing line. Bautista Agut has other ideas and gets the break back and manages to take the set 7–5, forcing a decider. Bautista Agut has battled back like the true warrior he is. He doesn't show any emotion except for when he breaks, has a valuable hold, or finally ensnares the fourth set to take it to that deciding set. He was seriously on the ropes at two sets to one and a break down in set four. It's a phenomenal fight back.

All to play for. Čilić again out-hits, on fire as he didn't manage in 2019. It's impressive form and, on this occasion, Bautista Agut cannot hold the Croatian at bay any longer. It's a vicious performance, from a marathon man, in a four-hour-and-ten-minute third-round epic.

Day of Shocks

Day five ripped up the rulebook in women's tennis as well as bringing some men's surprises along the way, too. In the women's draw, the defending champion fell, as well as everyone's tip for the title this time around, sent packing by players in the form of their lives.

Coco Gauff proved her worth with a breakthrough, which would become famous, by beating the brilliant Naomi Osaka and booking a surprise spot in the last 16. This came only hours after many people's tip for the title – and her record-equalling twenty-fourth Grand Slam – Serena Williams succumbed to the sword-like racket of Qiang Wang (6–4, 6–7, 7–5), who, only months earlier, had been knocked out at the US Open by Serena with a scoreline of 6–1, 6–0.

Milos Raonic had Stefanos Tsitsipas on the ropes. Big time. He led by two sets to love with everyone awaiting a Greek fightback. However, the deficit looked too much to claw back, not to mention how well the Canadian was playing (and Raonic did indeed win 7–5, 6–4, 7–6), putting out the seed who has ever-growing expectations surrounding him. Raonic will face Čilić in round four (a contest Raonic would go on to win in three tight sets) and that should be a cracker.

Roger Federer was again troubled by John Millman, playing in his own backyard, as he did a year and a half ago at the US Open (look up that stunner!) He broke Federer in the first set, led 4–1, then 5–2, and served for the set at 5–3 only to be broken back. Federer then served to level and was uncharacteristically broken to hand the set to the Aussie. Such occurrences normally sharpen Federer's instincts, and he then recalibrates and brings his most clinical game to the court. It was a rather topsy-turvy start. But Federer then stayed with Millman, and the pair went to a second-set tie-break that Federer easily won to level the match at one set all.

Federer and Millman continued their duel into the night. Federer took the third and Millman fought back, broke, and served out the fourth, leaving us all with the salivating prospect of a final set that would inevitably go past midnight and bring one man the spoils and the other the heartbreak. At 1–1, the players exchanged service breaks, with Millman unable to consolidate his break of the Federer serve, losing his own straight after in another mini-tussle game with several deuces. The final set went the distance too, and a tie-break to 10 decided it, with Federer prevailing.

Similar swings in momentum took place in the tie-break to ten. Millman was up 4–2 at the first change of ends and, in true Federer style, just would not bow, would not fade away, would not submit. At 5–4, Federer threw everything at Millman, and the Aussie took it, won the two service points, and took a 7–4 lead putting all the pressure back onto Roger's shoulders. An insane passing shot from Millman put him at 8–4. Federer with his own mini break for 8–5. 8–6. The match slipped into its fifth hour, closing in on 1:00 am in Melbourne. 8–7. 8–8. Federer back from the land of the almost dead. And then Federer won it 10–8 with six points on the trot. Millman should have buried it having led 8–4 up. But he wasn't playing a normal human being. Anything but.

Roger Federer simply will not be retired by anyone. Four hours and three minutes and he is into the last 16.

While the outcome wasn't a shock, it came awfully close on a highly memorable day for the Australian Open, both in 2020 and in the tournament's entire history. In fact, the history makers are at it again.

DAY 6

The Circus Is in Town

Nick Kyrgios gets his column inches. And some. His tennis warrants some of it. It's a shame about the rest. What comes with some rather spiffing tennis is a circus parade that is to the detriment of the sport.

At times, it's hard not to think that Kyrgios is his own worst enemy, a master of his own undoing. It'd be great to only write about his tennis, as that's his profession, but that isn't going to happen for this player. Yes, we need characters, but not rebels who want to burn the book of tennis on a global stage and watch the fading embers of the sport that gives them a comfortable living.

At the sit-down after the fourth-set tie-break in his match against Karen Khachanov in the third round – which goes the way of the Russian to level the match and push a deciding set – Kyrgios spends the whole sit-own shaking his head. Is he in denial about the score or how poorly equipped he is for professional sport? Or has the penny finally dropped how *extraordinarily* lucky he is in his life?

In another classic third-round match, Khachanov takes advantage of the weaknesses in the Kyrgios armour and, despite facing match points in both the third and fourth sets, he forces an unlikely final set. Kyrgios plays some great tennis. In waves. He also entertains, attempting tweeners (in-between the legs shot) – not always pulling them off – getting a time violation, bleeding, finding himself on the wrong side of the net to give

Khachanov a towel, and so on, and Dramaville has enough storylines for an age. The tennis somehow feels secondary. Khachanov gets his head down against a partisan crowd and carves out games and sets in the end, until he has given himself a shot. It's his workmanlike approach that keeps him in the match.

Kyrgios, at 40–0 down on the Khachanov serve and 4–4 in the final set, starts showboating and hitting tweeners. He knows the game is gone. It's pure swagger.

Khachanov probably deserves to win. He hits the reset button well after each set, every disappointment within the match, as Kyrgios dwells on every negative moment, inventing many along the way. That doesn't always prove the vital difference, and Kyrgios finds a way.

The final-set tie-break is the ultimate example of mistakes and brilliance as both men exchange multiple mini breaks of the other's serve. It's an incredible performance from both men and for such different reasons. Khachanov stands firm and stays so cool in such a wildly noisy and pro-Kyrgios environment that he should qualify for a medal of some kind.

Khachanov has his chances, but Kyrgios just manages to see him off. Something had to give, and the crack appeared in the Russian tower who had done so well to get back into the match. On another day it could have easily gone the other way. Kyrgios will face Rafa in the next round. What's the Australian English for '*ooh la la*'?

DAY 8

Wawrinka v Medvedev

Stanislas Wawrinka and Daniil Medvedev are tied at one set all in their fourth-round match after just over an hour of play. Plenty of service breaks – two apiece – and some hefty tennis being seen, dazzling the eighth day at the first Australian Open of the new decade.

The encounter turns into the somewhat inevitable five-set match it had written all over it. Medvedev claiming the third set to lead 2–1. Wawrinka then wins a tie-break set to force a decider. Grand Slam best-of-five-set matches really are special.

In the final set, Stan gets an early break and pushes on backing it up, Medvedev's clock ticking ever louder. After 3 hours and 17 minutes, he has two more break points on the Medvedev serve to get him to 5–2 and to serve for the match. The first falls by the wayside. The second, too. Wawrinka's chance isn't gone though, and from the second deuce he seals another impressive break of serve, Medvedev failing to convert his own game point. It ends with Wawrinka pushing through into the quarter-final to face Sascha Zverev, winning 6–2, 2–6, 4–6, 7–6, 6–2. Some vintage Stan there for all to see.

The Obituary of Kyrgios's Australian Open 2020 Run

The run of Nick Kyrgios at the 2020 Australian Open has passed away. While it showed some great signs of life until late in the day, it was not to last, Rafael Nadal ending the run in four sets.

The run will be remembered for a stunning five-set third-round match played out with Russian colossus Karen Khachanov – who came back from two sets down to lose in a final-set tie-break – and Kyrgios in some mesmerising form.

Lorenzo Sonego and Gilles Simon had previously been despatched before the third-round highlight. There were antics at every turn, much as there often is, in front of a home crowd salivating for more of their man's box office entertainment.

The body of the run to the last 16, much like the serve a couple of times today, is broken, and there will be a post-mortem to establish what happened and what can be learned. For learning is all we have.

DAY 9

The Openness of the Women's Draw

On any given day, at any tournament, one woman might win it over another. The ladies' tennis events have become increasingly unpredictable. While three of the six women left in the draw are past Grand Slam winners – Ashleigh Barty, Garbiñe Muguruza, and Simona Halep – there are three women left (half of the quarter-finals were played today, the other two tomorrow) who are new to this – Sofia Kenin (having reached her first ever slam semi), Anett Kontaveit, playing Halep tomorrow, and Anastasia Pavlyuchenkova, who has reached the quarters of all four majors and never gone any further. To say the ladies' event has thrown up surprises would be an understatement. Many voiced their belief Serena Williams might finally clinch her twenty-fourth and record-equalling major. Who foresaw defending champion Naomi Osaka tamely succumbing to wunderkind Coco Gauff? And what of Elina Svitolina, Karolína Plíšková, Belinda Bencic, and Kiki Bertens going out in a variety of exit performances ranging from damp squibs to close calls.

DAY 10

Kontaveit No Match for Halep

In this kind of form, there are few players who could handle the force of Romanian dynamo Simona Halep. While she may not win the ladies' event, she has shown a great side of herself thus far in Melbourne. Anett Kontaveit, in her first major quarter-final, may have hammered top-tenner Belinda Bencic 6–0, 6–1 in round three, but she provided no test for Halep.

Halep's lethal wand-like racket was able to steer Kontaveit all around the court, wielded expertly, with no mercy, and one singular mission. Having claimed a second major last year at Wimbledon, and with the return to her coaching team of Australian maestro Darren Cahill, not to mention players like Serena Williams and Naomi Osaka having long since departed the draw, things might just be aligning for the Romanian to finally find herself on the winner's podium of a hard-court Grand Slam tournament.

Kontaveit has undoubtedly made strides forwards with her game, but one of the best measuring sticks to see how far one is from the top is Halep at her best. 6–1, 6–1 is an impressive scoreline in any round, even more so in a quarter-final of a Grand Slam. Kontaveit may take a lot from the harsh lesson.

As for Halep, well, only Muguruza in the semi and then Sofia Kenin or Ashleigh Barty in the final would stand between her and a first Australian Open crown. It's a way to go, but in this form, there are few people who can match her. Muguruza and Barty are also on fire.

When Sascha Met Stan

Sascha Zverev's Grand Slam record is improving. In his first ever Australian Open quarter-final, he faces the gritty and surprisingly resurgent Stan Wawrinka. Stan will forever be famous as a man who managed to win three majors in the era of Roger, Rafa, and Novak. It's no mean feat. It hasn't left much room for young players such as Zverev to push on, silencing early and rather large expectations.

In the first set, Wawrinka overpowers a Zverev lacking any rhythm 6–1. Zverev then gets into the groove he needs on serve and at 4–3 breaks Stan, moments later serving the set out – 6–3 – to level the match at one set a piece.

It's good to see the German at this stage of a slam again (he has twice before reached this round at Roland Garros – 2018 and 2019). He is yet to pass this test and make a semi-final berth.

When Zverev breaks Wawrinka at the start of set three, he's clearly ascending, growing in confidence, finding his best tennis. He is then, however, broken straight back. At 2–2, Zverev makes another breakthrough. 3–2. As he pockets the set 6–4 to take the lead in the match and then breaks in the first game of the fourth set, it becomes clear that Zverev is now completely outplaying his far more experienced counterpart. It's an incredibly assured performance by the German and, whoever he gets in the next round, Dominic Thiem or Rafael Nadal, will have their work cut out with a version of Zverev so able to tap into his best tennis. Finally, it's coming good for the German, closing in on a thoroughly impressive victory and that first Grand Slam semi-final spot. He does indeed win, no danger to threaten his brilliant performance, a supreme showing. The scoreline is 1–6, 6–3, 6–4, 6–2. After the minor blip of the first set, Wawrinka wasn't allowed to even come close. Much more to come from Zverev.

DAY 11

Federer v Djokovic (50)

It speaks volumes about both the quality of returns early on as well as both men's lack of rhythm that there are immediately looks at breaks of serve for each. Roger just holds and Novak is broken to love. 2–0 to Federer. Djokovic – as is so often the case – then gets the break straight back.

It resembles an end-to-end football match that spawns endless talking points. Both men continue with issues on serve, but Roger breaks again for 3—1 and almost again, but not, and leads 4–2 and then holds for 5–2. A fascinating opener, the viewers gasping for breath, the majority, as might be expected, leaning towards the Swiss player.

I'm not sure I've ever seen it before, but serving for the set at 5–3 Roger is broken to love. The advantage lost, back to being on serve. Djokovic serves at 5–6 down and a few minutes later we enter a tie-break. The set starts with the feeling that Federer has much more time and is harrying Djokovic, preventing the serve from finding any fluidity. As the set progresses, it feels like the tables turn. Djokovic wins the tie-break with some ease.

That first set felt crucial, as though Federer's only hope in the match was to clinch it. It's hard to see a fightback now, especially considering Federer's long matches in the past rounds and the injury he sustained to his groin in the quarter-final that clearly greatly impaired his movement.

The second set is more routine, mundane, predictable, though of course there are some cracking shots and some almost breaks of serve, until at 5–4, serving to stay in it, Federer's serve is naturally pounced upon by his Serbian opponent. He breaks to take a 2–0 lead, and the match is done and dusted when Novak breaks again and then serves it out for 6–3 in the third and a straight-sets win.

DAY 12

The Zverev Breakthrough

It's been a while coming, but the three Masters titles and 2018 ATP Finals win went some way to suggesting that the hype surrounding the younger of the Zverev brothers, Sascha, as a sizeable part of the future of men's tennis was justified. However, that crucial Grand

Slam breakthrough eluded him. With each year you could sense the frustration. Despite reaching the quarter-finals at Roland Garros, over the last two years it just hasn't happened as the world might have expected.

In his final major before turning 23, has Zverev truly arrived? Reaching his first semi-final in Melbourne (or at any major) is noteworthy, but making the final is something to write home about; a giant stride in larger terms, not just of his tall frame swiftly covering the court. When he goes down two sets to one against Dominic Thiem after leading by a set to love in their semi-final, it reeks of being a step too far – his first major final – on this occasion as well. Zverev starts to lose his cool, unable to make challenges deep in the third set as he has run out of his allotment owing to poor challenges earlier in the set. It irks him and it's visible as his temper starts to fray.

A tie-break in set four is settled the same way, with Thiem proving too strong and finding his way past the German and into his first Australian Open final and third slam final overall. For Zverev, it is undeniable progress. Not the giant leap he might have wished for. Nevertheless, it's something wondrous to build on going into the remainder of the season and beyond. If he keeps playing like this, that breakthrough that sees him in a Grand Slam final – and even winning it – surely cannot be far away.

DAY 13

Women's Australian Open Final

Sofia Kenin has crashed into the Grand Slam winners' circle with a shocking and brilliant performance over a more experienced player. The 21-year-old American was a child prodigy and has now converted her early promise into something truly special.

She turned around a one-set deficit by beating Garbiñe Muguruza – 4–6, 6–2, 6–2 – and proved herself on the biggest stage, while sending a message out to the rest of the tennis world as she burst into the world's top 10 and looked every inch a deserving winner.

DAY 14

Men's Final

Dominic Thiem grows into the first set – and the match – and comes back at Novak Djokovic. And some. He breaks to get back on serve in the seventh game of the set after somewhat predictably being broken at the beginning by his experienced Serbian foe. Novak crushes the renewed belief of his opponent, as he always does, and breaks serve, soon taking the set for a lead that many would deem impossible to overturn.

Thiem gets an early break in set two, but as the set progresses you know Djokovic will break back and, of course, he does to level at 4–4. The odd thing is that he is then broken again for Thiem to take the advantage in the set again and he serves at 5–4. Thiem holds this time and levels the final at one set apiece.

When Thiem breaks Djokovic on the second opportunity it feels like something big is happening. Djokovic is ranting and raving and performing his usual ugly routine, blaming everybody in the vicinity – the crowd, umpire, etc. He sees himself as beyond the law and that it excuses whatever behaviour he likes on court.

Thiem breaks again (should that be in bold or italics, maybe?) – in an increasingly odd affair – and holds the Djokovic tide off. He serves out the third set 6–2 for a surprising lead.

Thiem gets close to breaking an out of sorts (or is he pretending again? It looks that way) Djokovic early in set four, but it stays on serve, and that might be huge.

Just as Conchita Martínez is a brilliant acquisition to the coaching staff of Muguruza, so is Nicolás Massú to Thiem. They have taken their games to the next level, made them better than their more recent incarnations. Remember, 2020 is just getting started.

However, Novak performs his well-known escape routine and does turn it around and take the match in five sets. While not an example of his oft-witnessed one-sided tennis, it was hard to see anybody bursting his Melbourne bubble of success. Even when he isn't at his best, Djokovic somehow finds a way. How do you approach playing him knowing that?

9 IN THE THICK OF IT
FEBRUARY 2020

Exhibition in South Africa

Nadal v Federer is nothing new. The location is one of the factors that makes today's exhibition match a potential standout of the month's action. Welcome to Nadal v Federer in Cape Town, South Africa. The billing as a serious match (after the light-heartedness of the doubles match with Bill Gates and South Africa's very own comedian and much more, Trevor Noah) is countered by the feeling that it doesn't have the same bite and passion that the pair's usual ATP or Grand Slam matches do. While getting to see these players in action is a must for many, it doesn't quite do the rivalry justice. By way of making money for the Federer Foundation that does so much good in South Africa (his mother's homeland), it's second to none in the tennis arena. This is tennis, but more than that, it's an occasion, it's something to remember, about garnering donations and helping a cause, using the globally recognised rivalry, and oddly friendship, to benefit those with less.

It's a match that (cynically speaking) could have had the result of the singles match determined prior to the commencement of the on-court action. On this occasion, the result counts for nothing. Or very little. It felt a dead cert that Roger would win in three (which he does) before a ball had even been struck (maximum time on court, to witness both men, the spark and fizz of their epic rivalry missing, replaced by a warmth of occasion, a camaraderie). Without the competitive fire or trophies on stands awaiting the victor at the end of it, it's hard to feel the same as we normally do, let alone for the two men on the court. You cannot switch on and off the extreme lust with which they take to the court in search of glory.

South Africa has been put on the tennis map in a way it hasn't been before; more than 52,000 spectators – a world record attendance for a tennis match – have seen something rather magical, and a sense of joy has lifted far beyond the stadium, up into the ether beyond the rafters. A memorable night and a reminder of just why Nadal and Federer are the two everybody loves.

Elena Rybakina's 2020 So Far

Elena Rybakina should be buoyed by her 2020 so far. Three finals – one as winner and two as runner-up – make her one of the in-form players, bull-like, making a charge for the top 20 and higher up the ladies' ladder. Her tennis is gloriously fluid and easy on the eye, with a big serve and shots that certify her credentials.

Her name infiltrated the draws of more and more events last year as her ranking ascended, and she's started the year by pushing the envelope of what she can achieve even further.

It's been a start to the season to be truly proud of. While she loses today's St Petersburg final against top-tenner and number two seed Kiki Bertens, she has made herself a hard player for most to beat. She's consistent, growing before the viewers' eyes, and has a game style much worthy of admiration.

Bertens becomes the first St Petersburg champion to successfully defend her title, and there can be no qualms as to how she merits this year's trophy. Rybakina, however, may feel disappointed at her return of one title from three finals, though something rather special is happening with her. Looking at the larger picture, it's massive progress and she's got the motor running, great distances yet to be (dis)covered. Rybakina is another player who really looks to be learning on the job, absorbing every second of experience, and using it to fashion a greater version of her tennis-playing self.

I, for one, cannot wait to see what the young Kazakh player accomplishes next. The sky is the limit, and 2020 looks all set to be a massive breakthrough year for her, memorable as it already is.

The Uneven Scoreline

Curiosity is sometimes piqued when matches have odd scorelines. When a player turns the score completely on its head, such as Anastasia Pavlyuchenkova did against number four seed Belinda Bencic today (the Russian Pavlyuchenkova winning 1–6, 6–1, 6–1), it reflects both the loss of rhythm of one player, and the discovery of something vital by their opposite number.

Losing the first set 6–1 – or by any scoreline – doesn't mean losing a match, of course not, but it does symbolise the need to snap out of a lull, slow start, or negative mindset, or else prepare to face defeat.

How many times have you watched a match or observed a scoreline where not only were the tables turned and a player managed to find their feet, where previously rhythm and time had been robbed from them, rendering them unable to make an impact, but the player in the ascendency managed to thoroughly thrash the rival when finally getting into a groove? I have the sensation I've seen it a lot lately, on score boards from tournaments I couldn't watch, as well as in matches I was able to catch. It always leaves me a little perplexed. Growing into a match is one thing, finding solutions. Yet such an extreme role reversal when losing the first set by a large margin is almost hard to believe.

It's perplexing to ponder the total change in fortunes. To see how a player can be so outplayed and then reset, start over, and do the very same to her or his rival.

Reversal of fortunes and execution of shots. One player stuck in the mud. Quicksand consuming them. Soon it will be over.

To analyse this more deeply, there are mind games and tactics for a whole match as well as a set alone at play here. Sometimes, players punch above their weight for a set and then cannot sustain that for a second and all-important set that would lead to a match win. Let's not even get started on the complexity of five-set tennis. The brilliant thing about tennis is that winning a mere set means nothing. While one step closer to winning a match, it guarantees nothing. If the other player keeps their head down and does what they are capable of, you'll be left wishing that the match was only a set long.

The Gilles Simon Crusher

Gilles Simon rolled back the years as he practically destroyed top seed and world number five Daniil Medvedev in front of a thrilled crowd on the Frenchman's home soil at the Open 13 Provence in Marseille. Not enough to knock out one of the event's favourites, Simon thrashed Medvedev, even delivering him with a second-set bagel to end the match earlier than many might have otherwise expected (6–4, 6–0).

Simon, now in the twilight of his career, is aged 35 and ranked 58 in the world. Once he was a staple of the top 20, even peaking at sixth in the world in January 2009, and anyone observing tennis closely will know he has been a very hard player to beat having been involved in some classic matches, reaching the quarter-finals at the Australian Open 2009 and Wimbledon 2015.

This win over a top five player will come as a brilliant boost to Simon's own title prospects here at the Marseille Open, where he won on two previous occasions (2007 and 2015). Simon would lose to Félix Auger-Aliassime (who would fall to Stefanos Tsitsipas in the final) in their tight semi-final the next day (7–5, 7–6), thereby failing to replicate his past glories in Marseille.

The Tale of Two Sets

While a set of tennis has parameters that cannot be broken, no match exploring beyond them, there are truly different possibilities. Take the ladies' Dubai Championships semi-finals today. Elena Rybakina beat Petra Martić in two straight tie-break sets in one 131 minutes. Hard work, a close shave, narrowly emerging the victor (Rybakina carrying an air about her that nothing she does lately is ever in doubt). Simona Halep also booked her place in the showpiece set for tomorrow by beating Jennifer Brady in straight sets. Halep's triumph, however, took one minute over an hour, less than half the time Rybakina's two-set win took.

The tale of two sets (winning in routine straight sets) doesn't quite do a match justice, as the content and closeness of those games and sets is what reflects the parity or gulf between the two players.

Rybakina will inevitably be tired after her recent outings on a tennis court and Halep is likely to be fresher and ready to send another final loss Rybakina's way. However, when it comes down to a match, what has come before does not always count as might be expected. Adrenaline and ability can go a long way to pushing us further than before. Halep might have expended less energy, but nobody this week, including top seeded players, has found a way to remove a lethal Rybakina from the draw. She's played a lot of tennis lately, even just today, but just maybe, at her age, it counts in her favour.

Rybakina would indeed go on to lose the final to Halep in three sets – 6–3, 3–6, 7–6 – succumbing in a final-set tie-break. Perhaps it was just a little too much tennis in the end.

The Roger Federer Operation Hiatus

Roger Federer is on a break. Possibly nobody wants to see that. Grass is hungry for more gliding from Saint Roger. Clay will miss out yet again. It is natural that a 38-and-a-half-year-old sportsman should need an operation to keep going. The unnatural part is what that same-aged body can achieve when fit and healthy. The dragonfly hovering, almost as if he stops time still, the butterfly floating, the tiger pouncing. All these things and more that we see from Roger as he poeticises the sport that we love.

So, a much-needed time-out to have an operation, a hiatus of sorts from the game, that will hopefully see the intended and plotted comeback for the grass court season, probably at his favourite Halle tournament, can be easily forgiven.

Perhaps this further indication of the end of his career is a cause for panic for the many fans and tennis aficionados the world over, but time will have to tell what Roger has left.

The Speech Is an Artform

Post-final speeches are a fixture of modern tennis that gives a voice to those victorious and those finishing as runner-up for the insatiable crowd to hear; everyone wants to listen to the sporting icons they follow all year round.

The runner-up gives thanks to all the people, sponsors, and figures you are generally now obliged to thank and then shrinks into the background, hoping to vanish from view as soon as possible, but is made to stand in the spotlight to witness the rest of the presentation ceremony. The winner gives thanks to the exact same people, their own team, and then parades a trophy before they too vanish from view. The key difference is the smile. One wears it, the other not so, barring some well-grounded and humble folk who can handle the loss. The speeches are mostly copy/paste jobs.

It's a testament to how curbed the instincts of those players really are, just how rarely a speech that stands out is made. You almost have the indelible feeling that if you've heard one speech, you've heard them all. The nod to the sponsors, the acknowledgement of the tournament and its chief organiser, to a player's team (and that of the opponent), and the crowd that pays the wages of the players. It's all so effortless, all so predictable and mundane, like a fixed fight or race. Only one outcome. The generic speech is as though a template from which you cannot stray, either read or memorised, almost like a national anthem, familiar, relied upon.

Occasionally, the template is shredded in true rock n roll style. See speeches by Li Na, Marat Safin, and Naomi Osaka as examples, as the true character of the person on the podium spilled out into the microphone, buzzing, and nestling in the ears of the excited audience. When it happens, it's a revelation.

Perhaps, much as with general life, folk are afraid to show anything of their authentic nature or are lost for words when the racket/tool used for their job isn't in their hand, doing the talking and standard communication is required.

We have words for a reason. Love or loathe her, take Greta Thunberg as an example. I'm not asking tennis players to change the world. But say something. Anything. Reveal something more than a factory line or parade of thank-yous that anyone could've expected far in advance.

10 THE PANDEMIC PAUSE
MARCH TO JUNE 2020

The Ghosts of Tournaments

Waking up to the news – on Monday morning of the week it was all set to kick off – that Indian Wells has been cancelled (nay, postponed some might say, though where on earth you can fit a two-week event into the calendar later in an Olympic Games year when it's already chock-a-block remains to be seen) is hugely disappointing. This would be just the beginning of Covid-19 pandemic-related tournament cancellations and postponements as the annual tennis calendar took a huge hit.

The players had arrived in preparation for arguably the year's biggest non-Grand Slam tournament. The public was salivating over the potential encounters as the women's game becomes ever more unpredictable. Along with the prospect of seeing likely champion Novak Djokovic and the players wishing for a slice of his success, unaware of what it takes (most of the field) to win a Masters 1000 event, and just aware that Novak is attempting a year unbeaten and to shatter every record in existence to smithereens.

Where once the stands at Indian Wells and Miami were loaded with excited tennis fans hungry for more action, they now stand hollow, empty, deserted. Different and challenging times were upon us and everything else – tennis included – was secondary.

A glimpse of what life would look like without sport is eye-opening. What we take for granted is no longer. A period of reflection – of indeterminate length – is upon us. We can ask what it is we take from the experience, what does it give us, what is life and how and where does sport fit into it? Can we fathom a world without sport?

When the familiar pattern is cut short, when an early ending enters from the wings of the stage, the emptiness howls. With the lack of tennis from early March now being taken through to mid-July at the very earliest, the splendid European clay and now grass court seasons of such vibrant colour and life abandoned for 2020, the new decade has denied us much of the calendar's usual proffering.

The tournaments during that period are hollow husks of their former selves, silent screams in the night. We know of them but cannot see nor hear them. They just are, existing in a limbo, depriving us of the entertainment that births so much joy.

The Disappointment of Wimbledon 2020 / The Ghost of Wimbledon

The one that got away. Destiny. It's hard not to focus on the fact that not since the Second World War has Wimbledon failed to take place on the golden and glistening green lawns of London's SW19, come rain or come shine. To be robbed of one of the jewels in the crown of the British summer sporting season is quite a big deal.

Simona Halep and Novak Djokovic will have to wait an extra year to defend those titles and everyone – always a year closer to retirement or injury or peaking – will lose one more chance to do something memorable, a feat of magnificence. Federer won't get another opportunity until the month before he turns 40, Nadal who was in very good form the last two years will miss perhaps one final shot, too. Serena, also in that club of the greats running out of time, edging ever towards the precipice of retirement. It will now come as nothing less than a colossal disappointment.

Where it would be was a blank canvas instead. It was the Wimbledon that was not to be. The white uniform outfits and the bodies they would not adorn, the teams and officials and ant-like workers all geared up for the same achievement – a shimmering summer sporting feast. It would be absent, a hollow vacuum where usually its riches would be submitted to all. The white painted lines that frame the court and its individual sections would remain unpainted, the paint unused, craving to leave its mark, a futile and ignored desire, a will unrealised.

The empty stands echoing sadness, the ghosts of Wimbledon instead, the present pining for the future when its voice can once again return to be heard. Perhaps longing for the past, for all that came true, for all that was seen, enjoyed, passed into memory banks forever.

Venus at 40

There can be little argument that as she turns 40 Venus Williams is a legend of the sport of tennis. While anyone else might have felt overshadowed by their stellar gifted sibling were she Serena Williams, Venus carved out her own space, led a changing of the guard, and redefined the parameters of women's tennis, only ever proud and supportive of her younger sibling's on-court achievements.

And she is still doing things on her own terms as she hits a milestone most professional players never do. The sheer love of the game is enough to keep her working hard and hoping for more victories.

There's no denying that Venus has been, is, and will continue to be a wonderful ambassador for the sport. She has won a great deal of the sport's prizes across both singles and doubles. She has earned everybody's respect and, when she finally retires, it will be an immense loss to the sport she loves so very dearly.

The Virtual Madrid Open

Given the circumstances, anything that cracks the mundane bubble of not having sporting events is something to be thankful for. With the Madrid Open cancelled, they found a way to put on an event with cyber followers (viewers from all over the world) as players at their own various homes dotted around the globe on various continents, rather than united by the European red clay, managed to compete via video link and PlayStation4.

Despite the clay not actually etching its familiar shade onto their tennis shoes and other sports gear, this time everything we saw on the tennis court was being ignited and inspired by a body, sitting at home, most likely on the sofa, and pushing the buttons of a remote handheld device, setting off the players, launching into serves and full-on forehands and backhands and, occasionally, volleys at the net.

Anything that can unite us is a privilege in these extraordinary times. The money raised will go to charity, which is only ever a positive.

The winners end up being Kiki Bertens and Andy Murray. Kiki defending her title (she won the real event in 2019) with what looked an intense and different kind of demanding. Murray, well, nothing he does surprises us anymore, but who would not revel in seeing him do it on the court when at last a return becomes possible.

Thank you Madrid Open, thank you PlayStation, and many thanks to everyone who enabled something so positive and inspiring in these darkest of times. Let us hope nobody got injured in the process and many had lots of fun with something different. It may not quite be true tennis, but it certainly filled the gaping void for a moment in time. Hopefully, next time around it'll all be much more real once more.

Volcano

Will it be as though nothing had ever happened? No more climbing up the walls, immediately it is forgotten. A rumbling can be heard, something is afoot, something is brewing.

Everything has kept quiet for some time. Enshrouded in a stillness, all calm and unspoken.

The wakefulness silenced. The motion paused. The stilled dreams and soundless hopes, dwarfed, suppressed. The volcano lies in wait, dormant, contemplating its surroundings, considering its moment, ready to pounce when the time is right.

From the earth with love. The explosion that unsettles and defines. When at last nature's voice is released from its cage, it would resemble molten lava spewing from a volcano. The rush, the burst, the intensely and immediately changed landscape. It had been sleeping, something growing deep inside, mutterings and rumblings, the only outcome to blow up. The only outlet release, the kind to leave a mark.

Nothing would ever be the same again, all kinds of blemishes and scars detailing the scenery, forever marring the memory, shaping the times. The destruction, the disintegrated harmony, the fleeting shards of hope stifled shall remain, the volcano reminding everyone that nature is all-powerful.

Missing Wimbledon

Wimbledon can be taken away from us. This time. When something lives in our hearts, however, it can never truly be removed.

The adage that you don't know what you've got until it's gone is ever apt. In troubled times it might do us well to ponder the magic of what we annually visit, experience, and bask in. Each ball struck is a unique piece of a giant puzzle that together makes any given fortnight at Wimbledon. That ball has been followed by numerous people both at the tournament and from other places around the world. Several of the Grand Slams are referred to as player favourites, but we all know deep down that Wimbledon is where it all began, and that kind of history cannot be replaced by any other brilliance. Add to that the sprinkling of so many key factors that Wimbledon elevates itself time and again above the competition, it's little wonder that the European summer has its annual crowning moment on the plush green lawns of England.

Pause for Thought

Tennis has only just got going again, albeit with a weaker field and the household names missing (a fact that claws away at the consciousness), and despite several American ex-tennis-playing professionals saying the upcoming US Open will be no less legitimate for the absence of many famous faces simply unable to put themselves, their families, and their teams at risk by travelling in this pandemic era, who are they kidding? Indeed, you cannot be serious. That these voices from past tennis champions share a nationality with Serena Williams, who is hoping to finally put to bed the infinite questions surrounding her ability to once and for all draw level on 24 major titles with Margaret Court, is an itch that cannot be scratched. The winners will count it as a major triumph, another added to their tallies (of course it is likely an existing Grand Slam champion will pick up the big prizes), they are victories that will appear in the records all the same, but nobody can be genuinely convinced that they pack the same punch, provide the same stern test as Nadal, Federer, and six of the women's top-ten players in the world are missing, not to mention many others.

No sooner than the sport has got itself back underway after a huge and unparalleled break, the social injustices off the court have driven us to stop play for the day, even to withdraw from the tournament and to pause for thought. Semi-final day delayed by a day would at first have no Naomi Osaka (she initially withdraws to show her support for the Black Lives Matter Movement), but as the entire event followed her lead and paused, she did play her semi-final the following day and won it (handsomely). People are throwing offensive comments about the (abhorrently stated in some quarters) need to whitewash Naomi Osaka's natural and beautiful human skin colour, and the bare truth of humanity both on and off a tennis court, out there in the world, is framed, shown off, and tragically, I assume, fed off.

Contemplate what it means to be good enough to be in the spotlight and then have to read and hear offensive language fired endlessly in your direction from the harmful minds that seem to spread through modern society like a plague. This language comes through social media and other platforms and gives those walking among us the tools for mental and emotional violence, a much harder issue to solve, to even see, than the physical violence that was more prevalent in the past. We want to talk about tennis. The larger picture, however, is getting considerably out of hand. We need to be proactive, to educate, to solve, to fight, and to love. We need to say 'NO!' We need to say, to show, to express that this is unacceptable and that every colour of skin, every nationality, and every sexuality is acceptable.

12 US OPEN 2020

The Five-Set Turnaround

Everyone – barring those in the camp of the player on the losing side and their idol – loves a good comeback. It stirs something in all of us. The almost-loser sparking to life and dishing out a lesson to the near-winner, punishing their failure to capitalise. Always chances in tennis, whether foreseen or not.

Not one, two, or three, but four men turned around a two-sets-to-love deficit to go on and win in five sets on day two at Flushing Meadows. The diamond in the crown of Grand Slam tennis – the five-set feast – once more put at the front of the display cabinet for all fans and naysayers to see. This would be missed if men's major tennis was reduced to best-of-three sets. These matches really get the competitive spirit inspired like nothing else. Andy Murray, Casper Ruud, Marin Čilić, and Karen Khachanov all saw the scoreboard leaning heavily in favour of their opponents and managed, through experience, savvy, and nous, accompanying the obvious talent, to convert the one-sided scorelines and end up in the first-round winners' circle.

That their opponents will feel extremely disappointed to have let such leads slip is neither here nor there, as there can only be one winner, and that's what makes men's Grand Slam tennis so very special.

Don't Panic, It's Serena

Some people – an extreme minority – know true magic. They are special, powerful beings. There is nothing you can do to contain their might, and the tennis court is no different when such a possessor of enchantments is present.

Did you see Serena Williams's trick against fellow American Sloane Stephens? All in good time, perfectly in her stride, no panic on display, she turned around the match with Stephens in a way that – despite how often she is still capable of performing such feats – merits the microscope treatment, the mesmerised analysis of artist eyes.

Yes, Serena turned around the match and made it all seem like she was the younger by a decade or more of the two players. She can do in her late thirties what most cannot do at their peak, because let's be honest, she is past her best and yet still reaching major finals, still clubbing as if her life, and those of her nearest and dearest, depended on it. She is still hungry and capable of going deep as those she faces run scared, even those players half her age with the confidence of youth if not experience on their sides. Time is of the essence, as English musician Paul Weller recently said, and Serena will know that sentiment well. As it slips away, as major number 24 (and finally drawing level with the great, but not particularly modern, role model that is Margaret Court) both beckons and withdraws itself from the realms of possibility, Serena is still battling like few others ever have.

I've written about the Serena effect before, that magical, seemingly never-ending, unstoppable curse laid upon other players. It scarcely ever fails.

The Passing of the Peak

Angelique Kerber may never hit those remarkable career highs of yesteryear again. Still only 32, she does appear to have left her best days behind. The younger crop is getting stronger by the day, while Simona Halep, Serena Williams, Naomi Osaka, Bianca Andreescu, and a couple of handfuls of other incredibly talented female players (at least) are all in the mix whatever the weather.

Kerber was outplayed, muscled off the ball, going for but not accomplishing her aim in the match against Jennifer Brady (in her home slam); the American hitting some lethal form.

Kerber will come and go again, perhaps believing she can yet replicate some of that past on-court majesty, but without any killer shot, just a tough, never-say-die approach, and shots that support one another rather than ever singularly devastating opponents. Is it not to snatch the breath away that she managed to win an Australian, US, and Wimbledon title, with only the French Open eluding her? At the beginning of any player's career, if they were offered those achievements, almost every player would snap your hand off and waltz into the sunset a happy woman or man.

...And Then the Extraordinary Happened

Finally (hallelujah and all that), Novak Djokovic's bad temper has caused him to be derailed. It's about time. He has long had a simmering rage at times, exploding and always appearing to go properly unpunished. Here is a man unable to comprehend the absolute necessity to face and accept both victory and loss, the two inseparable forces. His reality does not coincide with everybody else's. He is a law unto himself to get to his prizes, unlike other players.

The rules state that any violent conduct towards others on a tennis court shall be punishable by disqualification, and the rules shall have their day.

Let's face it, Djokovic was as much of a shoo-in for the title in Flushing Meadows – especially in the absence of his two greatest foes Federer and Nadal – as perhaps anyone had ever been, and maybe he himself felt that a little too greatly. It has something of the karmic about it when someone who frequently throws a fit when everything does not go their way and is dumped out of the tournament with the rule book playing master, having the final say and showing Mr Djokovic the 'exit' door. No name is as big as the sport.

That any type of discussion ensued – let alone an approximately ten-minute one – with the player pleading to be kept in the draw – is strange, to say the least. The rules apply to everyone, others having succumbed to this rule before, not simply the players who are less than excessively rich and who have never reached the heights of top of the world. Was Djokovic arguing that he should have been considered above the rules? It does smack of him having entered the draw in New York (and many other destinations) with that mindset – one deeply harmful to both the game and society.

What makes Novak Djokovic spectacular is his tennis. What ruins that and any chance he ever had of being globally adored is practically everything else about his behaviour on a tennis court. Always frustrated at playing bridesmaid to everybody's two favourite male players, he has coped with his excessive desire to be the most adored very badly. Your heart must prevail in those fragile and tentative moments, and in most cases, Djokovic's temper is what shone through, not his kindness, warmth, and love of the sport. In fact, to so readily taint the sport with regular bouts of on-court aggression, you cannot help but wonder if he really loves the sport or is just exceptionally talented at it. If that is not clear by now, well, it probably never will be.

The disqualification has done nothing to help his image, his popularity, or his final Grand Slam tally.

Now It's Interesting

This, then, is what men's Grand Slam tennis looks like without the Big Three. On the cusp of the second week and the only member of the untouchable trio to attend this year's Flushing Meadows major in New York is out in disgrace – in the ugliest possible fashion. There is a wide range of responses, though most stick to 'it's the rules', a hollow apology follows, and the dust settles – or rather blows up and does a joyous dance in mid-air – and the waiting younger crop still in the draw watches on, dumbfounded, mouths gaping, mathematical equations taking place in their brains, all thinking 'now is my chance'. You can almost hear them bristling with excitement.

Mothering Wednesday

How often does a meeting of mothers in the latter stages of any sporting event take place? The US Open quarter-final is a wondrous occasion for two mothers to face one another for a place in the semi-final. While one of the mothers, Serena Williams, is no stranger to this end of these events, still striking the ball with passion, wisdom, and endless desire, the other is much less practised at this phase. Not completely though, as Bulgaria's Tsvetana Pironkova once reached the semi-finals of Wimbledon. That was back in 2010.

Pironkova goes a break up and consolidates with an impressive hold for 4–2 in the first set. Serena by sheer willpower explodes into life to hold her serve again for 4–3. The match is already hotting up. Forget the absence of fans, if the tennis is good, you don't need mad crowd volume to verify that. Pironkova would go on to win the first set but lose the match, unable to get in the way of Serena's apparent latest date with destiny.

The Elder Statesmen Are Gone

Not only are the Big Three now absent – and how odd does that feel? – but there is no Andy Murray, no Juan Martín del Potro, no

Stanislas Wawrinka, or Marin Čilić, just younger players. The Big Three (all in their thirties), perennial attendees at this late stage of the majors since, well, they all turned 30 and continued what each had started in his twenties (even earlier in Nadal's case), are somehow all absent now as the US Open reaches the real nitty-gritty, revealing the promise of the future.

And in their absence, the young players step up to the plate and some rue the missed opportunity – Stefanos Tsitsipas, Karen Khachanov, Borna Ćorić – and some revel in this sparkling moment to truly propel their careers towards the stars. Dominic Thiem, who just turned 27, and Pablo Carreño Busta, 29, are the most senior members of the final men's eight. Carreño Busta has once before had a deep run to the semis at this major, and Thiem is a three-time Grand Slam finalist (and runner-up all three times). Alexander Zverev has reached one previous major semi-final, at this year's Australian Open. Shapovalov's previous best was the fourth round, also in Flushing Meadows, three years before. Andrey Rublev had also seen his finest moment by making the quarter-finals back in New York (in 2017). As for Alex de Minaur and Ćorić, their finest results had come by reaching major tournament fourth rounds (Ćorić on two occasions and de Minaur once). Medvedev was last year's runner-up to the irrepressible Nadal. It's hard in such circumstances not to lean towards the more experienced of the eight – Thiem, Medvedev, and Zverev, though who would bet against Rublev.

Tennis will continue long beyond Messrs Federer, Nadal, and Djokovic, and the other brilliant players of the era, too. But it's hard to escape the sensation that Djokovic had done us all a favour by performing a brilliant disappearing act from New York. And what of the race for most majors? It was not an example of shooting himself in the foot, it was an example of being caught, as what he did, he has been doing his entire career. He has chosen to walk a tightrope running the risk of exactly what happened in his fourth-round match in Flushing Meadows. If you are a Federer or Nadal fan, or even a fan of better on-court behaviour, you'll have been laughing, maybe still will be. For the sake of the young players having a good, clean crack at the title, this is the best possible outcome in the absence of the greatest two men's players to ever take to the court: yes, a Spaniard and a Swiss.

Azárenka Back from the Wilderness

It has been a long road back from giving birth to her first child and, having recently contemplated retirement, Victoria Azárenka has reached for the stars once more and found herself about to take to the hallowed turf of a Grand Slam final again. This time, her losing opponent in today's semi-final is none other than fellow mother Serena Williams.

Serena scarcely troubles herself to attend the coin toss; the mind games have already begun. She leaves the court briefly before the first point and it's as if she's telling her rival, it is her territory. The antics have commenced.

Serena pockets the first set and then misses a chance to go 2–0 up in the second. From thereon in, Azárenka joins the party and puts a seemingly injured Serena to the sword, pushing her out of the event, once again, without her much sought-after silverware.

After Words…

Azárenka is right. She wants her tennis to speak first when she is on a tennis court. She is a warrior who makes her own destiny, and not a mother weighed down by that role, though she would be happy to inspire her young son watching from the wings, as well as other people all over the world. She wants to be seen as the woman she is, with the ferocious attitude and bombastic swagger defining what she does in her job. She is not using parenthood as a talking point or reason for this, that, or the other, the two aspects of her very much separate in her own mind. While motherhood has clearly brought her wisdom that can translate to the tennis court, her comeback road had been a seriously arduous and challenging affair, requiring much patience. It is now paying dividends.

The Quiet Storm

The two women in the best form since tennis returned last month meet for the second time in three weeks. Well, in a manner of speaking. The first encounter was an absent match, an empty pod where something memorable should have existed, as Naomi Osaka had pulled out before the Western and Southern Open (W&S Open usually in Cincinnati) final leaving Victoria Azárenka the winner without hitting a ball.

Such occasions and their disappointing endings always bring the curtain down on events in the least favourable way. It had however birthed multiple questions about the two women who had reached the final here in New York to set up a salivating encounter between one of the young and inspiring new figureheads of women's tennis – Osaka – and a more seasoned ambassador in her Belarusian opponent, Azárenka.

This final, perhaps making up for the disappointing recent W&S Open no-show (also played in New York on these same courts), did indeed live up to its billing as a grand close to the ladies' singles event – the first major final during the continuing pandemic. Azárenka exploded out of the blocks to collect the first set 6–1, before Osaka ignited her fire, and her scorching play was too hot for the older of the two to handle. She surged to the finishing line, winning 1–6, 6–3, 6–3 to win her second US Open title (along with that infamous title, and first major, she claimed over Serena Williams in the New York final two years earlier).

These finals, their silent noise, so utterly unique and contrasting to what we have grown used to experiencing at Grand Slams and other big tournaments, will be long remembered if this year's second half and its tennis events are outliers.

The Finals

In the men's final, Dominic Thiem wrestles with some stark inner demons in the first set, perhaps his own greatest enemy here. Alexander Zverev seals the opener with an ace.

There is no crowd, but Thiem feels the pressure, of expectation, of Grand Slam final number four and potential history, and no collection of the trophy in those finals before. No Nadal or Djokovic on the other side of the net. Now a lower-ranked player. Thiem knows he should win this, has the experience on his side, and to add insult to injury, his pal Zverev is four years his junior. Pressure cooker.

Naomi Osaka had flicked a switch the night before and from a losing position suddenly accelerated towards a victory, finding that magical formula needed to win a major, and collaring her third Grand Slam title in the process, rather than allowing Azárenka to do so (both women had gone into the final on two majors apiece). Would Thiem be able to perform an escape special, as Osaka had yesterday, leaving her opponent for dust. There is plenty of time for a shift in fortunes.

Perhaps Thiem is missing the crowd and Zverev is revelling in its absence – remember how they distracted him in the past? Zverev closes in on the second set, even has three set points, and before you know it, they are gone, he is broken, and 5–1 becomes 5–4, Thiem entering the contest fully now. Zverev has one last chance to serve the second set out and take a huge leap towards eternal glory. Is he now thinking about things when he was not before? Zverev's tennis is not flowing quite the same as before. Don't show Dominic Thiem the doorway in. It would be a huge mistake. Danger is averted, and Zverev holds serve to take the second set and leads by two sets to love over almost everybody's big favourite to win the match today, Thiem – the weight of expectation making its impact? It's an exceptional performance from the young German so far.

When Djokovic comically sabotaged his own chances of further major silverware it was hard to look much beyond Dominic Thiem. As a three-time Grand Slam runner-up and the number two seed playing some incredible tennis it made most sense. None of that mattered and little of it could be seen on this quiet Sunday evening inside the Arthur Ashe stadium in New York.

Dominic Thiem does what he can and scraps his way through the next two sets to level the match at two sets all. It is as unexpected as the way the first two sets went, and it means either man could now realistically still win the tournament.

Finally, Zverev serves for it at 5–3 in the final set, having found his feet again after being sucked back to level pegging. Zverev is, however, broken to 30, choking on the opportunity. It's a tight and nervy game and could perhaps be him letting the match slip away, having been in command several times.

Neither man can win it though, and Thiem also fails when he has a chance to serve it out, meaning the match and the championship will be decided by a tie-break.

Swings and roundabouts, momentum ever shifting, a tie-break proves one last chance to push over the finishing line for one of these men. Both are struggling, neither can take the initiative. The shots are tentative, the silent atmosphere palpable, the weight of what is at stake here felt by all. Thiem fails to convert two championship points, the first on his own serve, but finally he claims it, winning the tie-break, the heart-wrenching decider that finishes off one man and leaves the other still standing. The Austrian wins his first major by 8–6 in the final-set tie-break.

Dominic Thiem is, for now, the more complete player of the pair and that is why, despite the huge lead Zverev had after two sets, the Austrian was able to turn it around (another example of winning from a losing position this fortnight) and claim his maiden Grand Slam title. The five-set format is absolutely a thing of beauty, separating these majors from their lesser counterparts in the men's game.

Thiem, for the first time in the men's modern era, comes from two sets down in a final to win a major title, completing the victory 2–6, 4–6, 6–4, 6–3, 7–6.

13 **FRENCH OPEN 2019**

Sinner Demolishes Tsitsipas in Italian's Backyard

A year on from their only previous meeting – a straight-sets win for Stefanos Tsitsipas, which had also taken place on the clay courts of Rome – Jannik Sinner had much more to say regarding the outcome. In fact, he showed just how far he had come in that year and change (as the Italian Open is being held in September rather than its usual calendar month of May), winning 6–1, 6–7, 6–2.

Number three seed Stefanos Tsitsipas was handed an on-court lesson by upcoming Italian star (and his junior) Sinner at this year's belated Rome Open, dishing out a beautiful defeat to his Greek rival today in a display that backs up his sparkling triumph at the NextGen tournament late last year.

Bar a blip of the middle set, it is a stunning example of his improvement and bright future. In a year when anything whatsoever can happen, the unusual is everywhere. Great strides from Sinner. Much more to come.

The Nadal Explosion

The clay court season – even if it is in September – can only mean one thing … Rafa is back! In a brief blitz over fellow Spaniard and recent US Open semi-finalist, Pablo Carreño Busta, Nadal showed his six-month pandemic-related break from the tour means very little and won't stop him quickly finding his groove again as we speed towards an autumnal French Open.

The first set starts with a slow grind and deuces exchanged as both men seek to do damage to the other. What seems tight at first turns into a rampant display from the King of Clay who collars set one 6–1.

Nadal crackled and surged like too much electricity in his opening match at the Italian Open. It meant nothing to the man that he had not played professionally in over six months, and he did not underestimate the talented Spaniard in front of him and taught him a clay court lesson (not for the first or last time in Nadal's life). How many of those remain? How many have been taken over the years? Can anyone even keep count anymore? Many superlative unanswerable questions abound. But he is back, and with a fizz, just in case it appeared it might not be so after such a lengthy delay.

Azárenka Sets Up Bagel Store

Handing them out at will, Victoria Azárenka is on fire hot on the heels of her run to the US Open final last week. From one player who when in her groove gets a strut going to another, Sofia Kenin will want to quickly forget this day (always a lesson in there somewhere though it might be painful to ponder).

Kenin will have nothing good to say about her encounter – her second-round match in Italy's Rome Open – with the currently in-form Belarusian Azárenka. Kenin should perhaps doff her cap to her opponent, give her a round of applause, or else some form of assigning credit where credit is due, with Azárenka coming out on top 6–0, 6–0 today. While everyone can have a bad day at the office, the player on the other side of the court still has to ruthlessly attack.

With not much left of a peculiar year, neither of these women would win another tournament in 2020 despite today's signal of danger for anyone awaiting Azárenka in the Rome Open draw (Kenin won the Australian Open early in the year when things still seemed normal, as well as the Lyon, France, event just before the extended pause to the season owing to the pandemic and Azárenka claimed the Western and Southern Open when Osaka pulled out of the final beforehand). So, the result will be remembered but holds no special weight, other than to show that on her day, Azárenka can demolish the best. Still. Her bagel store may only have been around briefly, but it was well worth a visit.

Roland Garros in Autumn 2020

You get so used to the annual feast of certain events that only when they are transformed or absent are you able to appreciate their majesty, their beauty, and their collection of little moments that will live on, making something far greater than the sum of its parts. Grand Slam tennis is a gift, coming in all sorts of shapes and wrapped with ribbons of many types.

You can feel the absence of the usual sparkling sunshine baking the glittering red clay courts of Paris. The colours and vibes are muted, and the players often look dishevelled by the conditions and minimal crowd. It looks like those familiar stands and courts, and yet everything is different. The tennis goes ahead, the world around it circling with fresh madness. We need the tennis to keep us all calm, to enjoy the season whenever it is being played.

Rublev Back From the Brink

Rublev, soaring after a triumph last week in Hamburg (only two days ago, in fact), shows his mettle and his endless determination not to be beaten. He's becoming everything he always indicated he might be and, despite having gone behind by two sets to love today against Sam Querrey, he was still able to find a way to take his place in the second round of the autumn French Open 2020. Rublev is one of the young players ever staking his claim for a seat at the big table.

A perennial battler who relishes the arguments you can have on a tennis court and the solutions a racket can find, Rublev surviving is a threat to everyone else in the draw. And as I write, Tsitsipas – the beaten opponent of Rublev in last Sunday's Hamburg final – has slipped two sets to love behind Spain's Jaume Munar, Medvedev is out, and not everything is as one might expect – the surprises keeping us all on our toes, on red alert for more upsets. One of the players of the year, Rublev, is safely through in the end.

Fighting for Survival

When playing in one's own backyard, players often feel an electrical surge of desire akin to in no other place. It pushes them to win and leave everything on the court more than ever before. Even in the days of a global pandemic – or perhaps expressly because of that – you can see how much it means to the French players performing on home soil and in front of a smattering of a 'crowd'.

You can feel it, the intense purpose, the graft to reach beyond oneself, almost begging fate, all set to deliver a losing hand, to reappraise its decision and reverse those fortunes. It's a phenomenal thing to perform on the biggest stages in tennis, and for the French, British, Australian, and American players to be fortunate enough to have such a privilege is irreplaceable, birthing moments to look back on years after the event and career have ended.

If you aren't fighting at home, abroad, every time you take to the court, well, what are you even turning up for? But, that delicious taste of winning at home, well, ask those who have done it, it's surely the sweetest of all feelings.

Tauson Time

One door closes and another one opens. Isn't that generally the way of things? Or, in this case, Caroline Wozniacki departs professional tennis and another Dane full of potential appears, making another memorable moment of day three, the first Tuesday of this year's entirely unique Roland Garros.

Sometimes one win on a Grand Slam stage is enough to garner attention and indicate a talent for the future. Seventeen-year-old Clara Tauson beating world number 25 Jennifer Brady 9–7 in the deciding set, in an almost three-hour match, is more than enough to make viewers sit up and take note. The young Dane convincingly demonstrated what her game is all about and has rightly caused a stir.

The 2020 French Open, already full of surprises, is keeping everyone on their toes. Just as Denmark seemed to have lost a great player, it looks like their tennis baton has been safely passed on to Tauson, making her presence known in a wonderfully intense and combative physical encounter, more than standing up to the challenge. Pulling off a victory such as this at the tender age of 17 can only indicate what may yet be to come from this young woman.

Zverev Has Ferrer Grit in His Corner

There's something about Alexander Zverev. Like he has finally dropped the shoulders, shed the weight of his and everyone else's expectations, focused on allowing his game to breathe and do the talking for him, and, maybe just maybe, found himself the right man to sit in his coach's corner to reap the long-predicted rewards. David Ferrer needs no introduction having only hung up his racket last year. But the exceptional, the extraordinary competitor that Ferrer was seems to have been transported into Zverev's game, and while the German's tennis is far from perfect, mistakes often render him consumed by longer matches than might ordinarily be necessary. Those traits that made the Spaniard so legendary on court are now leading and saving Zverev. It's clear to see and has not taken long to impact on Zverev. His great escape getting greater by the tournament as that well-known Ferrer grit sees him through.

Zverev has tried a few other coaches in recent years, accompanying his father in the coaching role, and neither of them worked out. Ivan Lendl and Juan Carlos Ferrero, well-known ex-players who could not transfer their successes to their relationships with Zverev. Despite Lendl's success as Andy Murray's coach, Lendl and Ferrero either clashed with or simply failed to get the best out of the Zverev boy, the younger of two tennis-playing brothers.

Ferrer, much like Nadal, was a player who was never out until 'game, set, and match' was called for their opponent, always believing a comeback could be on the cards and working single-mindedly towards that target when losing, and heading straight for the light at the end of the match tunnel when leading.

The young German who has himself been around for some time – at still only 23 years of age (and as some of you will remember last year inflicted upon Ferrer the final defeat of his career at the Madrid Open), has found the spark that was missing, has re-fashioned himself as someone able to come back from the brink of defeat, has grown up, and is implementing a new and much better mentality on the tennis court. His recent US Open runners-up place was no fluke and is surely the start of things to come. While he seemed overly arrogant in his earlier years, he has worked out what is important – playing tennis and improving, considering the near endless variables, and working on what one can do to control them, to keep results in your own powers.

His first-round Roland Garros win was routine. The second-round win was anything but, as he ground out a final set clincher against one of the home favourites, Pierre Hugues-Herbert. The Frenchman had a substantial number of chances and will rue the day for not taking them, but Zverev, despite not being fully at the races, finds himself in the draw for the last 32, not Herbert. That is what the top players do. Those wins give you the experience to dominate lower-ranked players on tough days at the office. The mental strength, the desire to prevail, the locker filled with matches of that ilk from which the elite of the game source confidence when it is most needed, when others might have it in short supply.

It looks, in its exceedingly early days, like a match between player and coach made in heaven.

Brutal Combat

Norway's Casper Ruud is joining the big boys. Despite losing to recent Grand Slam winner Dominic Thiem (here at his favourite major, Roland Garros) in straight sets, Ruud gave an indication of what we can expect from him in the coming years, and how he might also improve as Thiem has through his twenties (culminating in finally pocketing a major title recently in Flushing Meadows), thereby conquering on the red dirt.

Ruud did not take his chances in the first two sets. It's hardly an uncommon trait of 21-year-old professionals as they learn to live on court against more seasoned pros, the heavyweights of the sport. However, enough was shown, the fight, the powerful hitting, and the room for improvement to imagine Ruud as a stronger and harder opponent to beat within the next few seasons in which he inevitably climbs the rankings and closes in on the top 10 and perhaps even higher.

Shock of the Tournament

The wide-eyed youngster Hugo Gaston has given the small French crowd what they wanted and knocked past winner Stanislas Wawrinka out of Roland Garros in the round of 32, even delivering a surprise bagel to the Swiss ex-major winner in the deciding set (winning 2–6, 6–3, 6–3, 4–6, 6–0).

The season of the shock is very much continuing as results take all kinds of unusual turns and leave us wanting more.

Not that anybody would particularly wish the affable Wawrinka out of any draw, but fans of sport and the world in general love an underdog, and today was no different as Gaston showed his mettle to unseat a player who clearly loves the clay of Paris where he first won a Grand Slam tournament and has fond memories of some of his finest career work.

Another Nadal Pummelling

Nadal is well into his stride at Roland Garros yet again. The unexpected longevity becomes ever more impressive, an extraordinary feat, and the still-growing accomplishment has no equal elsewhere in sport.

His straightforward defeat of Italian world number 74 Stefano Travaglia puts him into the second week in form that will have the other men quaking in their tennis shoes. It's impossible to see past Nadal, Djokovic, or Thiem as the 2020 Roland Garros champion come Sunday week. Isn't Nadal supposed to be finding the conditions in October and the new balls harder? He just makes it all seem so effortless, and if you ask those who have won a single slam or even a couple, they will tell you what an incredibly hard task it is and why they didn't regularly repeat the experience. Logging another Nadal pummelling of a player at the French Open is standard now, an annual task, and something that has almost become mundane, but behind the routine lies the fact that with every win he snags, this is becoming an achievement in tennis and sport that no woman or man will ever even come close to touching.

The Altmaier Surprise

Coming through qualifying at a major tennis tournament is reason to celebrate in itself – let alone the opportunity to get one's teeth into the ensuing main draw with exciting possibilities at every turn – but many are confronted with much stronger and more experienced opposition in the early rounds, where there is no easy encounter, and those runs are not continued into the first proper week of the event.

Daniel Altmaier is one of the chief surprise packages of the 2020 French Open, and has now booked his place in the last 16, lining up with some of the cream of the crop of men's tennis. This is indeed a huge breakthrough. The young German can forget the inevitable ranking climb and financial benefits, and focus on playing and winning in one of the four most well-known stages that tennis has to offer.

When he breaks the Matteo Berrettini serve in set three of the pair's third-round encounter, and is only three games away from a shock straight-sets defeat of the sturdy and impressive Italian, it begs the question – what else can happen this fortnight in which Serena has withdrawn, young players have started to appear left, right, and centre, and Paris has been lit up in the autumn instead of the springtime?

Did Berrettini underestimate his young qualifier rival today? It wouldn't be the first time a better-known player automatically assumed he or she would despatch of a lesser-known athlete. Perhaps it was not that but other factors of which there seem to be so many of late that came into play. A humbling defeat for the Italian, a wander into unknown terrain for the German who has now played and won six matches, including the three wins in the qualifying event. He will relish a fourth-round tie against none other than Pablo Carreño Busta.

At the Net

Some of the finest tennis – and the best hands – you'll ever see will take place at the net, however allergic to venturing there some of the sport's athletes may be. It is an essential weapon, net play, and those who are well-armed will no doubt use it occasionally or a little more often to dramatic and spellbinding effect.

There is much to admire about the way players club the ball from the baseline with fluidity and consistency, attempting to discover new angles to bring them an advantage over their opponents, but I've always had the feeling much beauty constructed on a tennis court relates to forays into the net and solid volleys, drop shots, lobs, and a range of shots that only the best possess. If a rally is a sentence, a great volley can be the definitive full stop at its end, the culmination of everything, an execution of the ball and with it the opponent's hopes and dreams of winning the point.

The Halep Humiliation

Top players are freakishly and frighteningly good at very young ages. They have something the others could only dream of. Here is a story of a gentle but clinical revenge. It's Iga Świątek turning the tables on Simona Halep from their 2019 Roland Garros encounter in which later an admittedly stressed and inexperienced Świątek failed to implement on court what her team had plotted and, overwhelmed by the occasion, only won one game in a frustrating day's work.

This time around, Świątek asserted herself from the very off, turning the screw of agony on Halep, making her pay this time, again and again, as Halep had seemed like the clear favourite for the title. Świątek walked away with not only the match and her first Grand Slam quarter-final berth but also with the ultimate revenge, sending Halep into entirely humiliating terrain.

For some of the best tennis you'll ever see played against Halep, look up highlights of this match. Świątek – with shades of Federer – as her net play, control, and finesse stun almost everyone watching. This is something special.

And it takes Świątek all of 1 hour and 8 minutes to practically reverse last year's result with a scoreline of 6–1, 6–1. Last year took Halep 45 minutes as she met Świątek, who was like a deer in the big stage headlights.

Tennis is instinct, muscle memory. Don't think, just play. Your natural game got you within reach, allow it to do the same now. Total belief. She knows she can win, 100%. It is an incredibly assured and accomplished win when she closes it out without hesitation or doubt. If you play like that, and this is no fluke, of that I am sure, with that sense of composure and on-court commitment and elegance, you will win the title in six days' time, Miss Świątek.

Sinner Joins Świątek as Teens Stamp Mark on Roland Garros 2020

Jannik Sinner shone on Suzanne Lenglen court against Sascha Zverev, with the Italian only growing in stature, confidence, and on-court presence, as he saw the German off in four sets earlier today.

He looked cool as a cucumber as he logged a hugely impressive victory over Zverev, a recent runner-up at the US Open, and booked a date on Tuesday with none other than Rafael Nadal, the maestro of the Parisian clay.

Sinner joins Świątek as two of the young rising stars on whom to keep eyes firmly fixed in the coming months and years, as their explosive and incredibly accomplished games, even as mere teenagers, surely put them in line to sit atop the thrones of some of the Grand Slam tournaments of the future. Who knows, perhaps even this fortnight? Let's face it, it's an odd edition of the tournament, taking place this time around. Nadal, however, will have plenty to say in a few days' time.

The Qualifiers

Mightily impressive wins have taken qualifiers – that's right, plural in number – into the final eight of a Grand Slam here in Paris in the ladies' draw. This cannot be understated as, along with the four wins in the main draw, these players have been boosted and buoyed by the three wins in the qualifying event beforehand. Seven wins in a row at a Grand Slam is no mean feat. In the main draw, that would give you the title, and perhaps making the quarter-finals having played qualifying feels almost as great.

Martina Trevisan (soon to be 27 years old) and 23-year-old Nadia Podoroska in the women's draw are deservedly creating memories that will last here in Paris. While some players have fallen that might ordinarily have prevented this from happening – and others have stayed away from the event – these are runs that will either ignite a surge up the rankings and accompanying confidence to remain there or else never be matched again.

Taking advantage of the situation – fewer top players than the average slam – is still not easy, and sniffing the opportunity could be distracting. The draw is still a tough one to traverse, making winning four main-draw matches a tough ask of anyone not in the uppermost echelons of the game, so these runs will be remembered and, of course, savoured by those at the heart of them.

The Gaston Breath of Fresh Air

Hugo Gaston, surprise French package of a new-look Roland Garros (contemporary roof over Philippe-Chatrier court, autumn, cold, the list goes on – hopefully it's a one-off, excepting the new roof) is a breath of fresh air, an absolute delight to watch.

Late in set three, as both men in this fourth-round encounter – Gaston and Dominic Thiem – have chances for a definitive break that will pocket the set (or match for Thiem, leading two sets to love at this stage), the Austrian starts to look worn out. Gaston's game starts to take its toll on Thiem. When Gaston does indeed win the third set, and rightly so, I might add, it's down to sheer graft, willpower, and self-belief. Age means nothing, just the moment in time, right here, and right now.

Gaston keeps drawing Thiem into the net as if he were on an invisible rope, an abundance of drop shots spraying off the Frenchman's racket.

Many come off and many put Gaston in a winning position in the point if not winning it outright.

Gaston, at 5–2 up in the fourth set, knows as well as Thiem that the Frenchman is in the ascendency, and forcing a deciding set would not only be a stunning achievement but to bet against him completing another shock victory – even more of one – would be foolish.

Gaston is caressing the ball, has it on a string, performing masterful points, constructing works of art across the clay. His game style is flowing and beautiful now.

At 3–3 and advantage Thiem in the final set, I cannot help but feel whatever happens here the young Frenchman has lit up the tournament, his home major, and given me – and many, I expect – a joyous feeling watching him play tennis. Gaston is broken, and he does not go on to win another game from there, but he has given Paris and the world watching a very special dose of what he can do. You are left with the distinct feeling that you can only hope to watch his magic hands again as soon as possible on the biggest stages.

On match point down, Gaston had sent a winning passing shot down the line that had everyone gasping in disbelief. Extraordinary. He had stayed alive a little longer, putting everything, quite literally, on the line.

Thiem wins in five, a brilliant match, and it was one of those matches that makes you want to watch tennis all the time, that reaffirms your love for the sport, and gets you excited for how it can make you feel. No, it is not like that all the time, of course it isn't, but when it can provide such delightful times, it's ultimately rather rewarding. One to remember.

Jam-Packed Day 10

In a jam-packed day 10 on Court Philippe-Chatrier, in which yesterday's carried-over fourth-round tie between Ons Jabeur and Danielle Collins kicks off proceedings, the lucky few who get in to watch the tennis are in for a treat. Jabeur is in unknown terrain, and Collins is echoing her semi-final run at the 2019 Australian Open, both women in splendid form.

Collins is increasingly vocal as the opening set advances, and Jabeur misses her opportunities and finds herself a set down. Collins, in the ascendency, might be able to attribute her clay court form to her latest alliance in the shape of new coach Nicolás Almagro, the Spaniard who retired not so long ago. Danielle Collins boils over with anger in the middle of the second set when things start to go against her, visibly swearing and all set to explode. Jabeur presses home the advantage and levels the match.

Jabeur produces her first double fault at 30–30 when serving at 4–5 down in the final set, and a point later, Collins has prevailed, reaching the last eight of a major again.

Then, Elina Svitolina fails to take a golden opportunity to win her elusive first major title, as the highest seed left in the ladies' draw, and is sent packing by Argentine 131-ranked qualifier Nadia Podoroska in the first of the quarter-final action. The Ukrainian was unable to stop the barrage and the march of the Argentine, who must surely love Roland Garros in the autumn. It's her best result at a major by a country mile. Previously, she hadn't got through qualifying apart from a first-round loss at the US Open in 2016. She now finds herself into the last four, in one of the stories of this year's tournament, with a semi-final date for Thursday booked. Svitolina will live to rue the day, having left her best tennis far behind. Or will she? I still have those odd words of hers – that she had nothing left to prove to anyone after winning 2018's year-end WTA Finals event – ringing in my ears. You can't say that until you've won a major, can you? Surely not.

Following that is the baseline slugfest of Diego Schwartzman against Dominic Thiem. At 4–4 in set two, Thiem fails to convert seven break points and Schwartzman holds a tough service game to be within a game of a two-sets-to-love lead. He had taken the opener comfortably on a tie-break.

Once again, the scheduling is a joke that seems designed to make those involved in the last two matches of the day – one ladies' contest and one men's match – suffer.

The Thiem–Schwartzman encounter takes over though, and as it stretches its legs into a final set with over four and a half hours already on the clock, it's clear it's an epic of brutal hitting. Surely, nobody could have expected it to take almost a quarter of a day as it hits and passes the five-hour mark. Schwartzman breaks Thiem and serves at 4–2 up in the final set. He holds and will have three chances, one on his own serve, to get the biggest win of his career and book a semi-final spot for Friday.

It's 8:40 pm when Schwartzman seals the win in five hours and eight minutes. It has been a spellbinding occasion even if the ensuing matches suffer.

Iga Świątek – the Halep giantkiller – soon finds her footing after a stumble at the start of the opening set and despatches of qualifier Martina Trevisan in two routine sets (6–3, 6–1) in 1 hour and 18 minutes.

Rather astoundingly, though I'm not sure why anything is now a surprise in an edition of Roland Garros taking place in autumnal October – and Świątek also asks if Rafa will still follow her match – in the year that is 2020, Rafael Nadal and Jannik Sinner finally take to the court at around 10:35 pm. It's weird and nothing like Rafa's adored and fruitful spring sun-baked conditions, seemingly cooked for him and him alone.

The match inevitably goes into Wednesday and eventually finishes with a three-set victory in 2 hours and 49 minutes. The first set alone took approximately 75 minutes and was won on a tie-break by Nadal. A hard night's work, even though the scoreboard showed straight sets.

The Early Pounce

Forget finding your rhythm and allowing your opponent to do the same or choosing your moment and going in for the kill. Pounce at the very start. A select few – the big cats of the jungle, like Roger Federer, Serena Williams, and Novak Djokovic – see the start of the match as the ultimate and immediate 'thumbs up' to take advantage of opponent nerves, of their potential feelings of inferiority, of being intimidated, overawed, and to punish them. Losing one's opening service game – whether serving first or second – can feel like suddenly looking up at a sheer mountain face, a handicap applied to the scoreboard with a mere few minutes on the clock, a near impossible climb ahead, chasing a dream that was only ever meant to be precisely that.

Staying in touch, holding serve and keeping things level, sticking to and doing the basics well at the start are key to not set oneself impossible tasks later. Only, accomplishing this is much easier said than done. Especially when some of the finest players are tossing their kitchen sinks at you to break your serve, your spirit, and your whole well-put-together tennis game.

The early pounce is something most dare not even dream of pulling off, having to find their feet in a match growing in stature, rather than believing from the first point that you can simply conquer. There are no other possibilities. And while there are no other possibilities, and it will always be so in sport, it's that mindset to match the undeniable ability that makes the greats exactly that.

Psychology of sports persons the world over is a more important prerequisite for success than it has ever before been, the strong mental side, even the mind games, as key an ingredient as any other aspect of the game.

Świątek – The Silent Savage

Iga Świątek has shades of Mr Federer as she effortlessly moves around the court and puts the points to bed quickly. There is a startling efficiency to the young woman's all-round game, which has never been better on show than in this fortnight.

Świątek on court is so assured, composed, and mature. Others could learn a thing or two from her about calm on-court behaviour and channelling talent in a conducive manner. Throughout this tournament, she has looked like a Grand Slam champion in the making. What swift progress she is making.

The winners literally fly off the Świątek racket as she looks like a ready-made title winner (and has ever since that thrashing of favourite Halep). It's sublime tennis in today's semi-final with qualifier Nadia Podoroska, who has no idea how to stem the Polish tide, but it's hard to imagine how anybody would have the answers. Quite simply, it's another majestic performance from the teenage Świątek. Everybody is now watching her, knowing she's special. Kenin or Kvitová will have a Herculean task on Saturday, and only Świątek herself can possibly destroy her chance of claiming a first major at the tender age of only 19.

It's tennis from another planet as she obliterates her semi-final opponent, Argentina's Podoroska 6–2, 6–1 as if it were not a last-four encounter in a Grand Slam, and she was just playing tennis on some local courts and hitting a hot streak. And this is exactly what makes this young woman precious. There is much more to come from her racket, a poet's way with words that she has when wielding it. The match lasts a mere hour and 10 minutes, and the qualifier's hopes and dreams of an unlikely final appearance are brutally silenced.

Świątek's touch and feel are exquisite. She doesn't make a sound, her celebrations are minimal but sincere, a muted style the game absolutely needs right now, with other starry characters basking in the limelight of not just their tennis but their entire lives. Here is a tennis player allowing only her tennis to speak for her and doing it in breath-taking elegance. This is the tennis player the world needs. No drama, no flamboyance, just heaven-sent tennis.

She has left a trail of destruction behind her this fortnight and nobody on earth would want to play her right now. Nearly every point ended abruptly, with a silent savagery that is almost unheard of in modern tennis.

Świątek's longest match out of six has lasted 1 hour and 18 minutes so far at this year's Roland Garros. What a difference 16 months (since the tournament was last held) makes. Someone will have the mission of the century on Saturday to stop this young woman claiming major title number one.

The Elder Statesmen Are Back (Again)

We have missed them before, back in the period between 2016 and 2018 when the trio took it in turns to get injured, take time out to recover, and come back, some might say, even better, hungrier, and more ruthless than they had ever been before. There was a renewed focus, the look of tigers in their eyes, only ever seeking more glory, that sweet winning feeling, record books altered forever, and everyone else left in their wake.

Now, two of the three men are back and ready to meet for the umpteenth time in a showpiece match, in the Roland Garros men's final on Sunday. Roger Federer has missed most of the year through injury, and Novak Djokovic's stunning shooting-himself-in-the-foot incident last month and Rafael Nadal's absence in New York meant that the 'other' party of players had a chance to finally get on the board; Dominic Thiem's Grand Slam tally now having a rather fetching '1' beside his name.

It's hard to quantify how much these guys were and are missed whenever absent. Perhaps not by the other players, but by admirers of the sport. This golden era will be looked back on with disbelief by those that witnessed it – it really has been that wonderful a ride.

Far Behind the Baseline

Standing far behind the baseline can pay incredible dividends. Standing in a potential no man's land can be taken advantage of by the better servers. If this masterful return isn't performed with the power, punch, and precision of placement it requires, the attempt will fail. Only the confident and the well-drilled will prevail with a tactic that can see the returner of serve so deep behind the baseline that TV cameras do not show the player hidden by the advertising boards.

Giving yourself that little longer to move towards the ball – and watch Rafael Nadal jump up to pounce on it, with ample time to get around it as the ball ever slows as it passes the net and heads towards him – to see what is going on, and then pounce enables the receiver immediately to attack. While few winners are likely to be hit from so far back, it does afford the time to decide where to go, eliminating the impulsive reactionary shot-making when on the baseline.

Last Four

If you look back over recent years, Argentine Diego Schwartzman, clearly unfazed by his opponent, has posed a tough task for Rafael Nadal regardless of the surface or even the court, and today was no different (having recently beaten the Spaniard in Rome). A first set lasting 67 minutes and including some gargantuan-sized games finally ended when Nadal served it out after three breaks of serve were exchanged, and he managed to maintain the vital one.

Schwartzman is never out of the match and even at 2–0 down he battles to a decisive tie-break in the third set (which proves to be the end of the match). Schwartzman has once again given an incredible showing come the final curtain. Regardless of the number of sets – a straight-sets victory 6–3, 6–3, 7–6 – he has pushed Nadal all the way. He has proven himself worthy of his semi-final berth and shown he is closer than most to toppling Nadal from his clay court throne. Others would love to know what his secret is.

The match lasts over three hours. Nine minutes over to be precise. It's a tough and tight contest and you can't help but feel Nadal is sometimes aided by his vast personal history on these courts (like nobody else can claim to have).

In another compelling contest, Novak Djokovic staves off the efforts of young Greek superstar-in-making Stefanos Tsitsipas.

The younger of the two finds himself down two sets to love, manages to pull himself out of the mire and back to level it, and takes it into a final set before then capitulating, finding he has run out of answers.

Tsitsipas withstands a barrage from Djokovic in set four, after finding a way to win the third set and the Greek is growing before our very eyes. Djokovic's experience and savvy is enough to see him past in the end, but you cannot help but feel the matches between the best of the young ones and the greats of the game are getting closer with each passing year. Next year could be a real page-turner for tennis fans everywhere.

Women's Final

A one-time slam finalist – and champion – Sofia Kenin faces a first-timer, Iga Świątek, in a lonely Philippe-Chatrier court. Świątek is a pouncing tiger from the start, and gets a break immediately after holding the final's first service game to lead 2–0. She is tranquil, efficient, and incredibly aggressive. An overwhelming charm and brilliance on court.

The performance of the teenage Pole early on is one of a player wise beyond her years as her composure and flowing tennis seem effortless. Has anyone told her this is the final of a major? In the early stages, she is thrashing Kenin much as she has everyone else in the tournament. Prior to today is one thing, to carry it into a first final at Grand Slam level is a different kettle of fish altogether. Świątek would be the youngest ladies' champion at Roland Garros since Monica Seles in 1992. Świątek leads 3–0.

Kenin makes a readjustment and holds. 3–1 down still. Then the break back makes things very interesting as we are back on serve at 3–2.

At 3–3 the women lock horns in a game that feels like it may hold the key to the set. The two women are drop-shotting one another and finishing points that way, looking at mixing it up, using a shot that has certainly seen a rise in use at this autumn French Open. Świątek holds to get her nose back in front and stops the rot of having lost the last three games in a row. 4–3.

Both players are quiet and focused, mature, and have elegant styles. There are few tantrums, as if this showpiece is played by those who respect the sport and came solely to play for a small slice of its history. It feels like a drama-free final in which tennis is the winner. The smattering of fans is treated to a beguiling contest between two of the newest additions to the sport's biggest stage.

They continue to do close battle at 4–3 as Kenin is almost broken. Finally, Świątek pulls it off after around 10 minutes. The tennis is absorbing, both the major and mini battles. It's 5–3 and Świątek serves for the set next.

Świątek isn't allowed to take the set as Kenin's returns are suddenly electric at the most critical moment of the set so far. Is Świątek starting to feel the pressure? 5–4.

Ah! The art of breaking serve. There have been many this set, and the final one is decisive as Kenin serves to stay in it, and Świątek snatches back control to lead by one set to love. 6–4.

Kenin takes the early initiative in the second set. It has three-setter written all over it. That break will settle her a little. She serves next, and gifts her service game to 30. 1–1. It looks like being a story of service breaks and, for someone come the end, missed opportunities. There are plenty here and holding serve is becoming a valuable commodity; a very competitive contest.

Świątek steadies the ship, Kenin's expression gives her turmoil away as Świątek closes in on a service hold there. The TV commentator calls it a 'classy' point from Świątek and it's the perfect way of summing her up. Kenin is starting to dramatically lose her calm. Świątek will be happy as she moves to only four games away from a life-changing victory. 6–4, 2–1.

Kenin sees the doctor on court. She then disappears. Świątek hits some serves to stay warm. Practices some shots without balls coming at her. Kenin returns to the arena.

Świątek breaks again, her rhythm not affected in the slightest by the extended pause, and she looks ready for her first major title. 3–1 she leads in the second. Holding serve is no problem again and she has won the last four games. 4–1. Two games away now from a first Grand Slam triumph at only 19 years of age.

Kenin is a broken figure, knowing she has no answers. Six other women before her this fortnight know exactly what she is feeling. Świątek's recent tennis is simply too good, and the woman who destroyed Halep has proven it's her time. Surely the first of many Grand Slam wins for the Pole is now looming. She is soon 5–1 up with another break and will serve for the Championships. Incredible stuff from Świątek. A joy to witness.

She serves for the match. Successfully. 6–4, 6–1. The title is hers, the breath-taking run complete. Remarkable scenes and the beginning of what could be one hell of a career.

In 1 hour and 24 minutes, Świątek swept Kenin and the clay aside to become the new queen of Roland Garros. A teenage conqueror. And … she didn't drop a set to get there. She joins Ostapenko as only the second unseeded player to win the Roland Garros ladies' event during the open era.

Men's Final

Novak Djokovic goes from 40–15 to losing his opening service game. An immediate mountain moves into view; Rafael Nadal with a masterful early lead to neutralise Djokovic's overuse of the drop shot. Djokovic looks lethal early on, but somehow Nadal stays cool and calm and either hits winners or forces errors from the Serb's racket. Nadal takes a 2–0 lead. The hitting from both men is firing on all cylinders from the very off.

Djokovic's first serve percentage continues to be shambolic. His shots are brilliant, his serve thus far letting him down, and Nadal has a look at two more break points. The first is vanished by typical Djokovic magnificence, but he can't save the second. 3–0 to Nadal. From the very inception you can see that these two men – now in their mid-thirties – are still by far and away the best two players in the world. The level of tennis is insane. Early signs show this final could be a mesmerising feast. Nadal staves off break points in the next game and once again holds for a 4–0 lead. Djokovic surges in the next game. 40–0 soon turns to deuce, though, as the Serb's errors flow and Rafa has another break point. There are 37 minutes on the clock already, which shows the match to be anything but one-sided, despite the scoreboard. Back to deuce we go. Nadal breaks again and then serves out the set to deliver Djokovic a bagel set. 6–0. A long way to go, but a very impressive start. Forty-five minutes on the clock.

The second set starts in more routine fashion. Djokovic gets on the board and the match has a different complexion. 1–1.

The relentless Nadal pressure then makes Djokovic crack again – for another break (6–0, 2–1 to the Spaniard) – and spectators must be starting to wonder what is happening. Despite Nadal's clay court pedigree, I think everyone was expecting a closer contest than the scoreboard presently reveals. It's too early to yet dream of that twentieth major title – especially for anyone who is sceptical and superstitious of the number 13, or who knows how Djokovic is never truly down and out – but Nadal has exploded out of the blocks at a tournament that should probably have been named after him by now.

The small crowd is being treated to another of those legendary clay court performances of the 12–time winner Nadal. It doesn't matter that this is taking part in the autumn, this court belongs to the Spaniard. It's extraordinary to contemplate that Nadal has only lost one game in the encounter so far.

Djokovic crumples when Nadal has advantage and it's 3–1. Nadal is a set and a break of serve up and, while it is not impossible to conceive of a reversal in the men's fortunes here, it is starting to look a long way back for the Serb. Another break takes the Spaniard to within sight of the second set. This is imperious Nadal. 4–1. He serves and it's 5–1 and a game from the second set. Djokovic manages a rare hold, and at 5–2 Nadal will serve for the set. When he wins it 6–2, it is hard – though not impossible – to work out how Djokovic could turn anything here around and challenge in the third set.

They changed the ball; they played in autumn when the conditions are much less suited to Nadal. They put the roof over the court and Nadal is never as good with a roof on. And still, he comes in waves of attack, owning this court and stadium. They set the finest player in the world before him – a man who had been defaulted from one match this year and won every other match. And Nadal was ripping him apart. It must stand as one of the greatest achievements of his entire career if he can finish this off here. Added to the fact that he will have finally caught Roger Federer – after all these years – and they will become tied with 20 major titles each, making it an extraordinary and unparalleled accomplishment.

The third set of the match is tighter until 2–2. Nadal breaks. 3–2. Is it decisive? He then faces a break-back point. Nadal stretches to a shot that Djokovic looks to have won and reaches deuce. Mind-blowing tennis from the Spaniard. Equalling that Federer record is getting closer. Djokovic then finally gets some success and does break back, levelling at 3–3. He roars like an animal. Djokovic then seems awoken from his Nadal-enforced slumber. Before he was muted, and now he is ascending. Djokovic leads 4–3 in the set. The Djokovic barrage continues but Nadal manages to hold him at arm's length and equal at 4–4. He is only two games from the win and yet it still feels distant. Will Nadal manage to get through today and the fortnight without dropping a set again? Let's see …

Nadal fights back, determined not to let Djokovic back in the door knowing how lethal he then becomes, and he gets to break point for 5–4, but has the door shut on his hopes and dreams? Djokovic leads 5–4. Two hours and 27 minutes on the clock now.

If Djokovic can break here, we will be into a fourth set. Nadal makes it 5–5 to 15 though, and even-stevens it is. Nadal breaks though on a double fault from Djokovic and will serve for his thirteenth title here.

Nadal gets to 40–0 and wins on an ace, sinking to his knees in cool celebration. He has his twentieth major. He equals Federer's record, which for a long while never seemed possible, but Nadal has made it a reality. Two hours and 41 minutes and Nadal joins the greatest sporting figures ever in history. It is also his nine hundred and ninety-ninth career win, and his sixtieth clay court tournament victory. The numbers are extraordinary.

Nadal then says in the on-court interview it's not about equalling Federer today but about winning Roland Garros, the event of his life, again.

And there had been none of the usual Djokovic shenanigans and histrionics almost as if admitting that he respects Nadal as an opponent far more than his other rivals.

And so … Rafael Nadal claims the unlikeliest (and yet likeliest) of wins – a thirteenth title at Roland Garros – proving that absolutely anything is possible, and the number 13 is not as grim as some might have you believe. The win was not unlikely because he has never been anything less than impeccable at this major tournament, just because computing such lofty numbers has never seemed necessary or possible. Here we have an accomplishment that will stand the test of time.

Anything but unlucky, Nadal's 13 proves it can be a number of fortune indeed.

⑭ NOVEMBER 2020

The Strange Year Ends

London is the venue – and the O2 once more – for the familiar year-end tournament, the ATP Finals. It comes as a greatly anticipated event despite having not been informed by the previous 10 months or so (owing to the pandemic-related activity), as it ordinarily and annually is. This is still the cream of the crop since January.

In a year best forgotten beyond the realms of tennis, the sport has taken the hit of the break between March and August this year and bounced back well. The finishing line is in London again and collects the best eight male players of the year in a field that provides no weak pairings and has every player wanting to go out of the year with their firework making the loudest bang. The year-end tournament often has winners who are not the usual faces on the Grand Slam winner podium (yet, at least). For example, the last two years saw Alexander Zverev (2018) and Stefanos Tsitsipas (2019) claiming the silverware.

Two men in their twenties lining up in the ATP Finals centrepiece contest means none of the Big Three are present. It is no longer what the future looks like – as I keep reading everywhere – this is here and now. This is tennis with two of its chief noisemakers of the last two seasons pushing their way into further terrain that marks them as men to beat for the remainder of the field going into 2021 – another clearly uncertain period for sportspeople and the world over.

Magnificent (Daniil) Medvedev (who recently won the Paris Masters title at Bercy) prevails – beating Dominic Thiem, the runner-up for the second year in a row – coming from behind for the second day running (as he did against Rafael Nadal yesterday). The only man, in fact, to come from behind all week, and saving it for the last two matches to be played of the ATP Finals in the O2 (this being the final year of the event in the English capital).

Mature, patient, and resilient to add to his power, unique style, and never-ending batteries, Medvedev must now surely be looking to win a first major next season or the following one.

Medvedev had put his all into the third match – an inconsequential one, as he had already qualified for the semis (which not all qualified players do) – of his group, and is the only player to end the week unbeaten having played the best of the best.

On the cusp of a new year, and perhaps another strange one, we all hope it will not be littered with endless emotional and organisational landmines, and that life might be allowed to return to some semblance of normality.

The Century Line

The battle lines have been drawn. The modern game versus the vastly rich history of a sport. The need to draw ever more fans and with it the monetary equivalent rise versus not only preserving but respecting and nurturing everything that it was, has been, and presently is. The need for a natural and not forced evolution.

With all these wonderings, and more, we find ourselves lost in thought regarding the sport of tennis. And maybe some of this feels like issues that are much bigger than just being about sport as the internet age has yanked us violently into the twenty-first century, and much of the knowledge and many of the teachings of yore have been executed, and thereby rendered obsolete.

And so ... tennis stands on a threshold, potentially to be imminently decided by the millennial and henceforth babies whose characters are more defined by the cyber life than the traditions of over a hundred years, as opposed to those big names – surely heading towards the ends of their playing careers – who have upheld, respected, and been defined themselves by the past of the sport and its ambassadors of the old days.

The idols of the game's present legends go back as early as the middle of the last century, maybe even earlier. The young players now breaking through instead worship and have grown up hearing about – not to mention watching – Roger, Serena, Rafa, and Novak. It's not just a generational gap, it's a leap across the centuries, from a hundred-plus years of tennis into a world with a substantially different outlook.

Everybody wants a shortened form of tennis to facilitate the dwindling attention span of modern youth – including everyone else this entails – and kickstart interest in the sport; life eating into our time like never before it has. The extraordinarily exciting five-set Grand Slam format has its anti-fans desperate to take it down. Not enough that this last bastion of the sport (see the thrilling battles of the past) has had sets reduced to tie-break endings – now at three of the four major tournaments – people want it erased entirely to accommodate their desire to watch more clearly defined and shorter meetings between players. More than three hours is obviously seen as inconvenient, regardless of the sacrilege they perpetrate at its expense. That the elders of the game found a way to allow it to exist without going on forever was a beautiful solution to a problem that created more problems as time went by. The uncertainty of endless matches posed a frequent dilemma to those in charge of scheduling and court times, not to mention when courts would finish action for the day, light a factor until more and more stadiums were fitted with floodlights to aid evening matches. Matches in a near perennial state of lockjaw can now finish with a respectful ending. But if we were to revert to best-of-three-set matches for the men at the majors as well, what astonishing tennis would be lost forever. It is not a question. It is a statement, a pondering to rue should it ever come to pass.

While the fading generation of legends would not change it, all it will take in future is the next generation to voice support of the shorter format and the change seems somewhat inevitable. Think back, any fan of men's tennis, and choose your favourite matches. It is undeniable that the large percentage would likely be five-set classics from one of the four Grand Slams or other tournaments that also used to be best-of-five. A best-of-three-set match can still be a classic, but we are almost talking different sports. And that is what makes men's Grand Slam tennis exceptional entertainment, events second to none, even in the sporting hemisphere.

I see every Tom, Dick, and Harry trying their hardest to invent a short form of tennis to entertain the day's youth and bring new fans, all while irrevocably shifting tennis away from everything it has been that made us all love it, in the name of progress, money, and bringing in crowds that don't love the sport. But the entertainment of a revamped game, only sharing the name in common, is akin to a man or woman with a makeover who is now unrecognisable from their normal self, the natural person they are – in the name of entertainment. Think of Federer's five-set conquering performances at Wimbledon, of Nadal's Roland Garros escapades, and how uncomprehendingly well he deals with the format and holds his own year after year. Think of all the classics where players came back from two-sets-to-love down, because they worked, never gave up, and earned those victories. And the rush is on. Everyone dying to be the sport's saviour. It does not need one. None of these ideas has gained any real traction because those who love the sport for what it is refuse, rightly so, to let go of what is a stunning game in the sporting spectrum.

Personally, I would go the opposite way. I would highlight that the Grand Slams are exactly that – grand, another level, rocketing players into the stratosphere by doing something mere mortal players cannot. I would make the women's Grand Slam tennis different from the other tournaments in the ladies' calendar. I would set it apart as the men's majors are from the remainder (see the piece 'My Women's Grand Slam Vision – A Proposal' later in this book).

Maybe the twenty-first century does want something different. Why must it always be shorter? In a hundred years' time, will matches need to be only 5 minutes long, to accommodate the ever-diminishing attention span because too much empty content exists at every turn diminishing the focus of man? Surely, we should be encouraging an emphasis on what we enjoy and on understanding events, rather than bowing to demands for drastic and damaging changes.

And as the younger guns now firing on all cylinders boot the older generation of clinging giants into touch, in the slowest and most stubbornly denied handing over of the baton ever, it's clear something is changing, whether it is what people want or not. Social media provides a platform beyond tennis for the newer generations, it is a distraction, and perhaps a wonderful podium for change of all kinds.

With the support that is out there nowadays, both mental and physical, players are stronger, fitter, and more able to extend their careers beyond what might have once been possible.

If this is the end of an era for tennis, and it truly is being wrenched toward something unrecognisably new, let us be thankful to have had four of the best players ever to have taken to the court and guided us from one century to the next – two of them active in the 1990s (Roger and Serena) and two of them active in the early 2000s – and give us a plethora of memories we will never forget, not to mention their mark on the record books of the sport.

The young players now live on social media, document their entire existences on there, and see their lives in the spotlight as more than just taking to a tennis court. Maybe that is why none of the young players on the men's side have yet won a major tournament. The five-set format stretching and revealing in its highly demanding criteria.

15 A PHENOMENON

DECEMBER 2020

The Serena Williams Phenomenon

If endurance is a key aspect, even the most important characteristic, of a successful tennis player, then Serena Williams would know. She has hollowed out many a rival over the years, driving them into the dirt, leaving them for dust. There must be players out there, somewhere, still haunted by nightmares of facing the irrepressible American. From her 1999 US Open triumph, launching her career into the stratosphere as a teenager to the 2017 Australian Open win while in the early stages of pregnancy, here we have an idol for modern times, a woman who strikes every ball as if it were a horror of the world that if punched correctly would annihilate it whole. The 21 Grand Slam singles victories in between those two above, the Olympic golds and other big titles, the doubles and mixed doubles titles at major tournaments and the way she has gone about it all has redefined the parameters of tennis, firing it into the future, others playing catch up ever since.

Post-childbirth, too, Serena has been a phenomenon. The American's unique brand of confidence and determination has seen her flourish and endure beyond what many might have forecasted. Expectations surrounding Serena are to her just further little targets to hit, tasks to complete, hurdles to overcome. No task is too tall. Tennis has taught her well – she has learned how to work with all kinds of different people and how to navigate situations of a more stressful variety – and she has repaid the sport, and some, with a longevity of passion and results seldom seen.

She has prospered, as has the sport. She joined names such as Court, Graf, Navratilova, King, and Evert and surpassed them, painting a new realm of sporting brilliance for all to gasp over and glorify, a queen lionised, worshipped, followed to the ends of the earth.

If Serena's over 20-year professional career was a collage, it would have more colour and life – including discernible highlights to catch the eye of anyone looking on – than most could ever even dream of. It would be a sprawling tribute to hard work and dedication in the traditional, conservative, and intense culture of tennis in which she has played a part in a positive shift in the diversity of players. Tennis is blooming, and it's in no small part down to Serena, her sister, and the Williams bulldozer smashing through barriers and preconceptions.

Despite the fanfare surrounding the heroine, the noise such popularity makes, Serena's bliss, her special place, seems to reside within the walls of the silence and focus of Wimbledon. There, at Wimbledon, she has claimed seven singles titles, six in the doubles partnering her ever-present sister Venus, and even an early mixed doubles title (she also won one at the US Open) with Max Mirnyi in 1998. Beyond Wimbledon, the vision of Serena taking to courts all over the world – with her constant red racket bag and her fleeting hairstyles – to find similar success at the other majors and larger tournaments is a stark one.

While remarkably installed in the history of the game, a legacy of breath-taking dimensions, Serena is still looking forward, contemplating what she yet wants to achieve. It's a perennial desire, a hunger to pounce, to devour, to savour, to banish all doubts, weaknesses, and mistakes, and succeed in the face of adversity. She relishes the on-court war that is yet to come, what the future might hold, battling it out with the next generation, continuing to push herself and be a part of the modern graffiti of professional tennis. Maybe it's never enough, and therein lies the truth behind a woman who doesn't know the meaning of retirement. One thing is for sure, when she does eventually go down, she won't go quietly, she will go fighting as ever she has done.

And the celebratory swirls, skips, and jumps post-victory on the tennis court speak of a love of dance, another vehicle requiring self-discipline and in turn aiding her at her day job. She is a compelling creature – a woman, a fighter, a mother, and a global superstar – of complexity and magnificence, rich beyond all imagination, and that has nothing to do with traditional wealth.

16 AUSTRALIAN OPEN 2021

When Young Gentlemen Do Battle

That it even comes to pass is a miracle. It is a feat of organisation, of planning and engineering, of battling the substantial barriers set before the event that we can seat ourselves and observe the first Grand Slam tournament of 2021, down under in Melbourne Park, unfolding before our eager eyes.

The highlight of day 1 was surely the feast of the young men, Denis Shapovalov v Jannik Sinner (who won his second ATP title only the day before). The pair displayed the good, the bad, and the thrilling in a sparkling late-night five-set tussle.

The absence of shenanigans should not be refreshing, but it's notable that two such young players, focused and hungry, play no mind games and let their tennis do their talking. This is as it should be, and as the match enters the fifth and final set – Sinner having taken the first set, Shapovalov finding his feet to win the next two sets, and Sinner coming alive again to level the encounter at two apiece – it is a fitting finale for two such talented players. As well as Shapovalov has played, I cannot help but feel if the young and rather masterful Italian had had a couple of days off after his warm-up title win yesterday before his first-round match here, he might have put in a rather different performance.

At 5–4, Shapovalov serves for the match and has match point. It's all visibly cagey and he does not convert it. A couple of deuces are exchanged, and on the second match point, the Canadian 21-year-old finally puts an incredibly tough first-round match to bed. And it's well after midnight in Melbourne, and most people's bedtime. In fact, as Shapovalov hits a final winner that strikes the line, it is 10 minutes shy of 1:00 am, and the smattering of a crowd has been rewarded by two young men for whom the future is earmarked. Sinner a little unlucky, Shapovalov with a deserved and hard-fought win. A player few would want to cross paths with.

Far From Ideal Preparation

It has been an unusual Grand Slam to come into has the 2021 Australian Open. It was pushed back by three weeks owing to quarantine rules and other adapted obligations for the event to ensure that the Australian people are safe from the continuing coronavirus pandemic that is much worse in Europe and other parts of the world. Therefore, preparation from many different corners of the globe has been hindered, changed, even reinvented.

For contrasting reasons, Angelique Kerber, Victoria Azárenka, Jannik Sinner, and Dan Evans have already been rather abruptly booted from the door marked 'exit'. The women having been the victims of the hard quarantine that meant they went two weeks without even being able to leave their hotel rooms, with practice an absolute impossibility. The men, having claimed titles at the weekend and coming into the first major of the year in form, but having had no turnaround before their matches, now the best-of-five sets, found wanting against opponents that on their days they would arguably both beat. To be or not to be. The question is whether you would take a small title victory in a Grand Slam warm up or roll the dice for a deep run in a major. How many times have those players winning events only the week before, mere hours before a slam kicked off, been rubbed off the draw board in its earliest rounds, owing to fatigue or too fast a turnaround with matches? Big players never play the week before, do they? The answer may lie therein, rather than with a need for matches up until the last minute.

Just as with the US and French Opens of 2020, something has had to give, and this major looks and feels different.

The Tiafoe Test

Novak Djokovic had his first real test of this year's Australian Open when Frances Tiafoe took a set and made the second round far from routine and rather a challenge for the Serbian boss of Melbourne. Tiafoe, long on the edge of a big breakthrough without seeing consistent victories over his peers that might get him into the world's top 20, is, on his day, a phenomenal prospect. At his best, he is also one of the best players to watch. That it all comes and goes over the course of a game, a set, and a match, and from tournament to tournament, is what prevents him from winning matches such as these, as well as his opponent's strengths and, of course, reliability to perform on the biggest stages at a level most can't even pretend to cope with.

In the end, as might have been expected, Djokovic did indeed pass the test, sending himself into the third round and nicely finding a groove that few have been able to disrupt in the Australian heat each year.

Meanwhile...

Over in Biella, Italy, at an ATP Challenger event, the recently disappointed Andy Murray is making his way slowly through the draw, heading to what will be an appearance in the final that he will go on to lose. His appearance at this year's Australian Open was snatched from him owing to a returned positive coronavirus test. He and his family were counted out, no workable solution becoming apparent, and he combed his options for some match action at the same time to take his mind off what he was missing: to get on to the court and do what he undeniably most wants to do – stroke those fuzzy little yellow balls and get match wins under his belt.

He has had to deal with so much adversity since he deservedly became the world number one back in late 2016, ending the year truly on top. His body had been burned out, his spirit undiminished, the physical side stealing from him a couple of years at least of competitive action that we all know he was capable of.

This year he will turn 34. What is there left? What can he still accomplish with his body less capable than it was before? Can he still manage magical Grand Slam displays that remind everyone of who and what he was? Can he come back fully, or most of the way, as we crave to see?

The Spiral

The spiral out of control can be seen regularly if watching a lot of tennis. Players with less-than-brick wall mentalities will be discovered, will be unveiled and will be breached. Belinda Bencic today, as Karolína Plíšková who lost a little earlier, performed like a woman not only bowing before but irreversibly burdened by the weight of expectation – her own, those of the people around her, and even her countrywomen and men back home in Switzerland. After Martina Hingis and Roger Federer, well, Bencic believes that the Swiss await her glory also. And it is visibly crushing her, as far from looking like a woman enjoying playing the sport and taking something valuable from losses as her temper ever frays, she appears far, far away from Grand Slam tennis dreamland, a place she has long since pictured. Now, that vision may not even be attainable to the still-very-young and unarguably talented young lady.

Watching the player spiral is hard, knowing it could be halted, certain it's simply a trick the mind plays on those sportspeople who are not as talented in the department of mental fortitude. It's a skill to acquire (see Świątek having a psychologist as part of her team) if not born with it as some are, and if you don't find a way to keep the demons at bay, you'll never become the player that your physical prowess and technical skill set would wish for. The full package is a far rarer thing.

It's a vicious spiral descending into the depths of failure – with each point your body becomes tighter, everything pulled taut, and navigating a path to solve the puzzle, to turn the screw on one's opponent looks decreasingly likely.

One Down, Two to Go

If Serena Williams pulls off winning the 2021 Ladies' Australian Open title it might be considered the greatest feat in the history of women's tennis. Don't bank on it, but don't bet against it. At 39-and-a-half years of age, she has just beaten Simona Halep in the quarter-final. She will now – the most likely outcome, at least – need to beat the other two of the best three players in the world if she is to claim the prize that she has sought obsessively for four years.

In more than just an epic grunting contest, Serena overcame Halep to finally gain revenge for their last meeting when the American lost in two straight sets to Halep at Wimbledon in the 2019 final.

It's the match of the highest calibre at this year's tournament, including the men's draw, so far. It became a match about the return of serve. Point after point was the absolute pinnacle of the event, almost shocking tennis, jaws hitting the floor as the two women did battle as only they know how; the level of decibels travelling across the Australian air like balls screaming past. It's mind blowing what they did today at one stage.

Serena came out on top, and she has one hurdle fewer, though they are likely to be even harder tests.

Recalibration Needed

Alexander Zverev and Novak Djokovic are in set two. Zverev won a very tight first set. All that hard work to take the opener, and then a loss of focus and execution and the ascent of Djokovic in the following set means the match is soon tied at one set all. Zverev, after finding the recipe for success contra-Djokovic, surrenders the second set with a whimper. Recalibration is needed, never more than when the Serbian eight-time champion has found his lethal groove and looks set to dominate anew.

There is little time in which to collect oneself, overthinking will lead to one's downfall. You need to be clever, somehow relaxed, and efficient. The list of qualities required, and the way every single jigsaw piece needs to fall into place, and quickly, can often make the task an Everestian one. Alexander Zverev, while perhaps being armed with all the tools, can't quite find the way past the ultimate roadblock, regardless of his ability to recalibrate during a match.

The Slow Handover

It's that time again. Rafa has a date with one of the best young tennis players in the world, and a fresh attempt to delay ageing, to silence the ticking, and to show the younger generation what really matters is heart. And nobody has a bigger heart than our beloved Spanish stalwart seeking that elusive second Australian Open title. It feels like it would have been – and still would be – thoroughly deserved if he did finally claim a repeat of 2009's victory. It gets ever harder to envisage though.

Things are all level for the first six games in the quarter-final with Stefanos Tsitsipas. Rafa then pulls away as he has been seen to do on so many previous occasions, preventing the grubby paws of time to manhandle and defeat him for yet another tournament in another calendar year. He is soon a set (6–3) and 2–0 up. It doesn't end there, Rafa, sensing his opportunity to finally reclaim the prize in Melbourne though a spectacularly in-form Medvedev, awaits in the semi-final for the winner today, as Nadal continues to push Tsitsipas over the edge. He breaks again, taking the second set almost out of sight of the Greek. Nadal will serve for it at 5–2 and a seemingly insurmountable lead by two sets to love.

As the clock ticks past nine o'clock in the evening in Melbourne, Rafa pockets the second set and it looks like an impossible ask for the young Tsitsipas to come back from this position.

The hammering, though, is arrested as Tsitsipas relaxes and retrieves his best tennis. Having shed the weight of expectation, he squeezes through the third-set tie-break, with Nadal making more mistakes – even an unusually sloppy overhead miss by some distance. In set four, it is more of the same as Tsitsipas grows and Nadal shrinks, and the scoreline shifts from one man to the other as weighing scales do when something heavier is introduced to one side with the other side previously having been the one weighted down. Every point is a world, with a moon orbiting it, the centre of the universe, all that matters.

The slow handover – years in the making – continues as Stefanos Tsitsipas takes the fourth set against Rafael Nadal in the pair's quarter-final encounter in Melbourne. Into a decider we go, a wholly unexpected outcome two hours ago – the whole match was turned on its head by a young Greek man suddenly able to neutralise Nadal's lethal threat.

That it culminates in one of the very few times where Rafael Nadal, after possessing a 2–0 lead, unravels and is beaten scarcely seems more than just a strange dream. Tsitsipas beat Roger Federer, at the time the defending champion, here two years earlier and went on to get hammered by Rafa in the ensuing semi-final, but similarly that smacked of change in the upper echelons. Now, it is another moment that feels like the end is coming closer, looming, a train approaching its final station, where it will be parked and left to grow old.

Has there ever been a handover quite so painstaking? The younger players frustrated for years at the refusal of their older foes to pass the baton on to them.

Nadal is spent, the Greek finding a way to complete a very special comeback for which he was speechless afterwards, and Nadal might be just a little closer to the realisation that that second title will never be achieved. One of the few goals of his career that has remained unobtainable.

It feels like the death of something, perhaps only small, but an ending, nevertheless. Rafael Nadal may now never win that elusive second Melbourne crown. He had his chances in finals against Djokovic (2012 marathon), Wawrinka (2014, injured), and Federer (Rafa led 3–0 in the final set in 2017), but was unable to take them. In his last final there in 2019, Djokovic thrashed him, as they had both done to every other man in the draw set before them.

Four hours and five minutes reads the match time clock on the court of an empty Rod Laver Arena, and that is how long it took Stefanos Tsitsipas to win against Rafael Nadal in the Australian Open quarter-final today. What happened over those hours and minutes is as odd as the fact that two of the world's best players were playing on one of the world's finest tennis stages to an invisible crowd. In front of empty stands and profound silence, the Greek turned a two-set deficit into a monumental victory that will be talked about for years to come – one of only a few men to ever do it against Nadal. The fake applause played over the speakers after points only served to augment the lack of noise, a hollow and yet truly telling setting for such drama in a world as troubled as it is right now. Beautiful tennis cannot be denied and, thankfully, however you look at it, we have seen a great deal of that in this match today.

The Battle of the Generations

When the best of the generations come together it is a moment to savour. Naomi Osaka and Serena Williams may not be meeting in the final in Melbourne, but nevertheless it is a match and an occasion – with fans back in the stands after a five-day lockdown – that will have many tennis fans salivating. This is a special match-up, there is no denying. Sixteen years and 20 major titles separate the pair. Osaka would seem the natural heiress to Serena's throne, and is the player looking most comfortable on the Grand Slam stage out of all the women capable of claiming major silverware.

It's a tantalising match, and from the very offset it has us on the edge of our seats. Serena gets to a 2–0 lead before Naomi settles into her rhythm and soon makes it 3–2, both with near endless chances on the other person's serve, exchanging glances, firework winners, and a smattering of errors. Osaka's groove is soon unbearable to her opponent, and she breaks to 15 to go 4–2 ahead of Serena. Osaka is making it look easy, and it appears the younger of the two generations is speeding towards the final, one foot striding forwards to take its spot. Osaka holds to love, and Serena looks dishevelled – not a word commonly associated with the legend. Serena's performance in the opening games today, and against everyone else in the draw thus far, had shown a woman rejuvenated and one with her destination thoroughly set for a mission to be accomplished – the impossible number 24 – and a date with history.

Serena, a little like Roger and perhaps soon Rafa, is in denial about the slipping, even vanishing ability to win the biggest prizes and beat the best young players, refusing to let go of what has been a shocking dominance over the past two decades. This time, and once again, it's just not meant to be. The number 24 just too big an ask, ever more elusive, with a young opponent made of what looks like similar stuff to Serena – something that makes it perhaps even harder for the American to take.

The first set is won in around 40 minutes, and Osaka then breaks Serena to drive home the message that it is her day. It starts to feel like she is teaching her elder counterpart a lesson. It is soon 6–3, 2–0 and Serena has won only one game since leading the first set 2–0. Serena holds serve, her first in some time, and is on the board in the second set. She must stop this quickly slipping away. Osaka is playing phenomenally fast and accurate tennis. It's swift, it's impressive, and it's as clinical as is needed against, arguably, the greatest woman to ever have played the sport. It's hard not to think that here, Osaka is showing everyone Serena's true age as most cannot. It continues on with each player holding serve and is soon 4–2, with Serena's clock ticking ever louder down on her.

Osaka gift-wraps a second-set reply break of serve to make it 4–4. Two double faults at 0–15 had given Williams three break points. Osaka had awoken from her lull too late, and it was all level in set two. Serena had won the game to 30. Osaka fires back and breaks Serena to love, a show that the outcome today is entirely determined by the young Japanese woman, and she will serve for a straight-sets win to book her place in the final.

Osaka goes 15–0 up. No weak game this time, as she rapidly gets to three match points and takes the very first, sending Serena Williams to her ending in Melbourne.

Serena will be thinking something along the lines of how there is always one frighteningly brilliant player standing between her and the trophy. Over the years, how many other women had pondered the same when Williams herself had been the unmovable obstacle? She is unlikely to give up just yet, but boy, is it getting harder by the major.

Naomi Osaka wins, making it all look rather simple – as the very best tend to – and it's hard to look past her winning the title on Saturday for the second time in Melbourne.

The Brady–Muchová Semi

A three-set battle unfolded earlier today between two women who might not have been expected in the ladies' Melbourne semi-finals – Jennifer Brady and Karolína Muchová. They were both on the side of the draw initially containing Ashleigh Barty, Belinda Bencic, Karolína Plíšková, Sofia Kenin, and Elina Svitolina. Nowadays, however, expectations of the women's field are futile, with shocks lurking everywhere. A surprising number in the starting line-up can get to the latter stages of these tournaments, and it is being proven time and again in recent years.

Brady uses her experience of the semi-final stage from last year's US Open against her opponent, who is a little more reigned in. She wins the opener, fails to quite keep up the level she has set, thereby losing the second and seeing it taken to a decider. The final set has shades of Thiem–Zverev in last year's US Open final, in that both players are so desperate to win that their best tennis abandons them and comes back in bursts and waves, and the struggle to the finish line lasts longer than it might ordinarily. In the end, the American seizes the moment, channels her desire into a fitting final charge, and accomplishes a dream of making a first major final. Credit to both women participating today. I don't think it will be the last semi-final berth for either woman. Brady wins 6–4, 3–6, 6–4.

Two Champions in Waiting

Daniil Medvedev and Stefanos Tsitsipas are undeniably two Grand Slam champions in waiting. One may even take the Australian Open silverware two days from now. The other will have to wait, though it's hard to see that it will be much longer based on recent form. Both men are getting better all the time, in the same way that Andy Murray, Stanislas Wawrinka, and Dominic Thiem did before finally claiming Grand Slam victories in the era of the greatest trio of male players the game has ever seen. It's no different for these two men; Tsitsipas having despatched Nadal so spectacularly (and surprisingly) in the previous round from two sets down. Medvedev isn't afraid of anyone, and has beaten the best players in the game repeatedly over the last couple of years, showing he may well be the next non-Big Three world number one and major winner.

Medvedev gets the first break in the first set of their semi-final encounter today and is soon up 4–2. He manoeuvres his opponents around the court as though they were chess pieces on his board.

Medvedev has just turned 25. Tsitsipas will be 23 later this year. Having witnessed Tsitsipas overturn Nadal's lead a few days ago, all this tournament needs is one of these men to beat Djokovic in the final – no small ask on the Serb's favourite stamping ground – for the handover from the legends to the brilliant next generation to look almost complete, especially on the more physically demanding hard courts. Making that final step is the hardest one though, make no mistake.

While the crowd is clearly behind the young Greek player, Medvedev is no stranger to being the baddie and revels in quashing the expectations of the cheering masses.

In set two, Medvedev having pocketed the first, the Russian gets a double break to lead 5–2, and what he is doing to Tsitsipas is similar to what Osaka did to Serena Williams yesterday – totally neutralising their power and majesty, taking away all their weapons. As Medvedev serves the second set out to love with an ace, it's clear this is a masterclass by the Russian. Medvedev has thus far comprehensively played his opponent off the court, giving the biased crowd in favour of the Greek little to cheer.

The score is soon 6–4, 6–2, 2–0, with another – and now probably critical – break of serve putting Medvedev close to the end of the match. It isn't the close five-setter some might have foreseen, but that it is such a (comprehensive) decimation of a talented young champion of the future only goes to say how ready Medvedev is to step into the ultimate limelight.

Tsitsipas, however, finds a break back after Medvedev fails to go a double break up, and they are suddenly level at 3–3 in the third set. The crowd comes to life, Medvedev is suddenly a little frazzled. Tsitsipas holds serve and the set wears a totally different complexion. Medvedev's seminar is on pause as Tsitsipas wrests the control for a handful of games. Medvedev emerges from his stupor and gets three break points at 5–5. He takes the second with an astonishing passing shot and reacts to the crowd that favours his rival, knowing he is a game away from a second major final. He does it in straightforward fashion, and he had clearly flicked the switch back to machine – magnificent robot mode – after being 0–30 on his serve when serving to stay in the third set. A timely return to his level from the first two and a half sets.

I'm not quite sure why crowds see Daniil Medvedev as an antihero; he's just what the game has needed, a unique game style, an icy exterior, the antidote to the era we are just about to emerge from. He is something new. He's a bright and funny guy, too.

Tsitsipas has had no say in the outcome here, Medvedev taking matters into his own hands, and that is how you win or lose matches, being the one who dictates, the one in control. It's frightening how good Medvedev has been today. He looks like the world's best player, and that is saying something. The new ice king looks ready to be crowned. Only the biggest obstacle of all remains in the way.

By the end, and despite a date with the substantial force that is Novak Djokovic on his favourite court looming standing in the way, Medvedev has never looked more ready or likely to ascend to the Grand Slam throne.

The Osaka Hurdle

Forget the rankings, Naomi Osaka is the best female tennis player in the world right now by some stretch. The rankings are shambolic, owing to the pandemic, and frozen points in the continuing tour have lent to a look that does not fit the reality. Nevertheless, it is undeniable who is the player to beat. Osaka is atop the perch of women's tennis and looks comfortably seated there, with the appearance of a woman who is not going to be budged, certainly not easily, for some time to come. She is the rightful replacement to Serena Williams's mantle. She is also the nemesis of that lady, who cannot find her twenty-fourth major with Osaka, and sometimes others, ever obstructing her course.

No matter how good Serena becomes again, regarding her fitness, her sharpness, the assault of her oft-witnessed power, if the Osaka hurdle is set before her, she cannot get over it in the key part of a Grand Slam. Perhaps rightly so. Should a 39-year-old mother be able to beat a 23-year-old who has modelled at least part of herself on one of her childhood heroines, namely Serena? Nature and logic present a compelling argument, undeniable facts at the root of their case, and ageing and diminishing in some sense is inescapable. Let's face it, it is not as if Serena has not been up high with a great distance to fall from the summit that she reached, a new peak for women's tennis, let us acknowledge.

Osaka has a tool chest of much sought-after equipment to get her into and successfully out of the biggest matches of her career unscathed, victorious, ascending. Her experience showed today; her savvy in these big match situations is unparalleled for the young modern players. She is the complete package.

Jennifer Brady comes in as a first-time finalist who might have nerves on her side, especially after the close of her semi-final with Karolína Muchová.

Osaka holds serve well in the first game of the match. Brady follows suit. The first break falls to Osaka not long after, and Brady gets a break back to see the halfway mark of the first set pass with parity on the scoreboard. It's an enticing encounter, with the sensation that it hasn't clicked into a higher gear yet as the two players weigh each other up, make mistakes, and bring some splendid tennis to proceedings. Anyone who expects Osaka to play Brady off the court is disappointed – the opening set is tentative, the unease filling every corner of the again now partially filled stands.

At 4–4, Brady gets a break point that would symbolise the end of the pair's closeness, but she fails to convert, Osaka pockets the game soon after, breaks in the next game, and takes the opening set. She then goes on a run of games that sees her quickly get to 4–0 in the second set, before the brave Brady fights back making the scoreline more than respectable, with the superior Osaka then finishing off the job for a 6–4, 6–3 win.

Both women give a good showing of their abilities, and Jennifer Brady should be immensely proud of what she has achieved this fortnight and just how far she has come in the past months of a troubled year.

Osaka looks the part. Brady was every inch a finalist who the tournament can value, and her first ever speech on such a big stage was confident, warm, and her words were wonderfully genuine. While the outcome is a surprise to nobody, it certainly provided a fuzzy feeling of warmth and appreciation for a tournament that might never have taken place. To all those that made it possible, it is hard not to be extremely thankful. Big tennis is tennis at its best, and yes, that is what we all wish to see continuing, even in these frankly bizarre and uncertain times.

The Japanese woman is the one to watch in ladies' tennis, having now won a major tournament in each of the years 2018, 2019, 2020, and 2021.

To Outfox Djokovic

To outfox the wily old Serb is some feat indeed, but to out-Djokovic the man himself is a magical phenomenon to marvel over. Daniil Medvedev, the latest finalist (for the second time against one of the Big Three) to fall short at this task, thoroughly warranted his spot in the final, albeit without causing any major dents in the armour of his older and tougher Serbian rival today.

All the pre-match talk alluded to Daniil Medvedev having little chance in today's encounter as Novak Djokovic is a machine and cannot be beaten, not in Melbourne, not on this court, not even when injured. The Serb has won eight out of eight finals in Melbourne thus far. He was hampered, it would seem, picking up an injury in round three and keeping a lid on that in the ensuing rounds, ever the secretive force unwilling to give anything away.

The Serb did indeed explode out the blocks, and two easy service games and an early break gave him a rapid 3–0 lead in the opening set. The Russian Medvedev then clicked into gear and got his own show on the road. 3–1. He then took Novak to break points and converted the second, and the one-sided scoreline was quickly back on serve. 3–2. 3–3, with a smooth service game from Medvedev. Now, it looked more like a final. Until at 5–5, things were without great drama. Djokovic held and got his foot safely into tie-break terrain (6–5 up), and, as he tends to, he sensed the opportunity – which at 5–4 down Medvedev had removed by holding serve in 61 seconds – and duly broke the Russian's serve with some spellbinding shot-making to lead by a set to love. Getting to the tighter lottery of a tie-break felt like Medvedev's best chance of getting his teeth into the match, finding himself a set up on the board. Alas, it was not to be.

Medvedev got a break of serve at the start of set two, and it was then followed by four games on the trot to the Serb. Medvedev, with an easy service hold and at 4–2 down, desperately needed to get the break of the Djokovic serve back. He did no such thing and the final, unfortunately, turned into something of an anticlimax from thereon in. Djokovic won the second set routinely, Medvedev making it all too easy for him by having a meltdown and never regaining his composure or his best tennis, rendering the 'iceman' nickname of recent days obsolete. The break of serve by Djokovic early in set three meant the match was not even a contest, everyone being robbed of the close battle they had hoped for, and which the first set had been.

Medvedev let himself and his followers down by being broken in such a predictable way; the mental strength of previous rounds and tournaments entirely absent after set one when put to the ultimate test, and his mask had slipped to reveal an at times petulant child. There's much more to come from him, but you cannot but wonder if he hadn't lost his cool and had continued to work as he does against most of his opponents, whether it might have looked somewhat different.

Sakkari Plates Lesson for Osaka

Naomi Osaka looked a heavy favourite coming into the Miami Open. On the back of winning her fourth major at the recent Australian Open, she has elevated herself to a superior plain in women's tennis, and to see her only take four games from the in-form Greek player Maria Sakkari is surprising and yet also a welcome outcome. The rich depth on the ladies' side of things has been part of its appeal in recent years, making it a sport to follow for the unpredictable outcomes since Serena Williams ceased winning the biggest silverware. The result today blows the draw wide open and offers a clearer opportunity to the remaining women in Osaka's half of the draw.

Sakkari will be buoyed by such a performance, one in which she was the aggressor and did little wrong. A match to build on and give confidence for all the right reasons. It's a little disappointing that the following round saw her exit. While incredibly close to following up her big win today, she would go on to lose in a final-set tie-break against the eventual runner-up, Bianca Andreescu (who would retire hurt before completing the final against Ashleigh Barty, who was back to her own very best form to claim the title again).

If Bianca Andreescu Is Fit...

... the rest of any draw had better watch out. A fit Canadian Grand Slam winner in Andreescu is good for the game and makes it a more competitive field than it would otherwise be. Players are going to be running scared.

... we might get a chance to see the rankings as they really are. If this last year has done anything – with frozen rankings – it has shown us the best players in the world over the course of a troubled year.

... we will find out just how good Naomi Osaka, Simona Halep, and the others really are on a hard court.

... there will be a chance to observe how she translates her game to clay and grass courts. Other surfaces pose unique problems to players – switching between the multiple surfaces fluidly is another achievement. She has not – since her ascent to Grand Slam winner – had an opportunity to play on either surface or grace Roland Garros or Wimbledon with her game.

... tremors may be felt in other locations, such is the ferocious power of the Canadian queen of the courts. She is a storm, a one-woman explosive, an intoxicating watch for anyone who loves the sport. She is a force of nature, in short.

... and finds her groove, there is every chance she will reach the latter stages of tournaments, as the number of players who can cope with her are rather few.

... there is every possibility of seeing her top the tree of ladies' tennis for years to come, or at least be in a constant tussle for that spot with Osaka and whoever else might appear in the coming years. Cori Gauff, perhaps.

… tennis will be as entertaining on the ladies' side as it can be. Andreescu possesses just the kind of character both on and off the court to elevate the game and bring in new fans. She is an essential presence for the game, and it can only be hoped she stays fit and healthy and delivers the kind of gritty performances this fortnight has been witness to in the future. We all know how some players are magnets to injuries. Let's hope she is not one of them.

Sinner Delivers in Roberto Bautista Agut Treat

Roberto Bautista Agut on his day is one of the world's finest players. If a little more consistent he would be well inside the top 10 rather than on its edge.

As he is presently proving – now a set up on Italian wunderkind Jannik Sinner in the pair's Miami Open semi-final – he has the tools to neutralise the weapons of magical young forces such as Sinner. Turning it on at the right moments and making his experience count he takes the first set after a very tight first 10 games. He broke and served it out. Simple. It was not so, but he made it look easy after having lost an early break and awaiting his next opportunity patiently.

It does not last though, and Sinner, who recently won the pair's first encounter when they met at the Dubai Tennis Championships in a very close three-set affair, proves he can hang tough with these players and then some.

Jannik Sinner is an extraordinary young tennis player. He has been bestowed with gifts from the tennis gods that most players would beg, steal, or borrow to possess.

He is just a braver tennis player than most, on top of his evident abundance of ability. He has no limitations and, frighteningly, will only grow from here. He levels the match and forces a final set. Coming from a break down in the deciding set, the way he breaks Bautista Agut to love to win the match is a thing of beauty.

Sinner is such a centred and impressive young sporting figure. The best players look something like this as teenagers. The kid has no fear, and that, for the other players, means pure danger.

Professional Parade

Ashleigh Barty swept Bianca Andreescu aside in a performance that pinpointed her right to claim her continuing number one ranking in a time when the global pandemic and frozen rankings have reflected anything but the reality of the last year or so. You might say Barty has a point to prove, though I expect she might suggest otherwise, cool, calm, and collected as she always appears. By defending her title here at the Miami Open – the first time she has successfully done so at any event in her career – she has made a statement as to what she is capable of when she finds her best work. In fact, the performance, short as it ends up being, is akin to watching a work of art. In full flow, she is a gifted player with a range of shots second to none. She has the full arsenal and uses it terribly well, resembling past on-court legend Justine Henin more than a little at times.

Watching Barty at her best, as on display this past fortnight in Miami, is like witnessing serene waves of the ocean lap upon the shore. Her tennis is beautiful, her composure constant, and her attitude on and off the court an example to all and a credit to everyone involved in her career.

In an impeccable match, Barty practically writes Andreescu off the court, the entire script in her hands, such is the extent to which she controls the points and their outcome. At 6–3, 3–0, and Andreescu having recently taken a tumble, it's hard to see how anything can prevent this match imminently meeting its ending.

A medical time-out ensues. Can it stop the rot? A game later it is over. Nothing changes during that game, and with Barty at 4–0, Andreescu retires injured. It feels a bit like Barty has physically broken Andreescu by moving her around and hitting ball after ball putting her opponent in constant motion until she could no move more.

The Polish Master

Hubert Hurkacz means business from the off in his maiden Masters final, serving first, finding an early break of serve, and soon putting himself in a commanding 3–0 with Jannik Sinner itching to get on the scoreboard.

Sinner then bursts into the match like an over-excited latecomer. He holds serve. At 30–30 he hits a brilliant winner, followed by a deep return to Hurkacz's feet that the Pole cannot return, and we are back on serve, the tantalising lead all but vanished. A short tussle later, it is 3–3 and parity for the first time thus far.

At 6–5, having broken to take the lead for the first time, Sinner served for the first set and lost it to love. He then succumbed in the tie-break, failing to take the chance, and then perhaps feeling the strain of the moment again. Hurkacz then completely outplays Sinner, always getting one more shot back, leaving the Italian flapping and without answers. Sinner looks incredibly frustrated as he slips to 3–0 behind in the second set, this time with the momentum even more against him.

Some immaculate tennis gets Hurkacz to 4–0 before a Sinner fightback and it is soon 4–3; the Italian doing something similar to the first set to get back in with a shot, although he is still a break down. It then proceeds with the server holding until Hurkacz serves for it at 5–4. Sinner goes down fighting in a manner that very few players – especially of his tender years – are capable of. 30–30 becomes 40–30, and Hurkacz wins a tentative final point to seal his first ever Masters title having just turned 24. In the absence of the Big Three, someone had to swoop in and steal the title. Hurkacz is absolutely worth his prize, and who knows where he goes from here.

18 A PROPOSAL AND CHANGE

My Women's Grand Slam Vision – A Proposal

Short forms of tennis keep popping up all over the place. Everyone wants to reinvent the sport, find something as amazing but in bitesize form for those with short, modern attention spans. Possibly, to the detriment of the sport, to draw fans of anything but what has made people follow tennis for over a century. Rebranding, redesigning, reimagining our lives and what they consist of makes sense, for so much around the world outside sport has changed, so alterations might bring it in line with where we now find ourselves in the contemporary sphere. However, is less more? Are short forms of a remarkably powerful, eye-catching, demanding sport the right way to go?

I have been wondering how we can get more and not demand too much without breaking the camel's back or destroying the soul of the sport. It means tampering with a winning formula. It also means denying history, though I strongly feel it nods in acknowledgement, doffs its cap to thee, the sport of tennis, a hero as it is.

I would make a women's major the best of four sets, and if it is level at two sets all then I would play an extended tie-break to ten.

Imagine this … the women at the Grand Slams play sets reduced to the first to five games instead of six (so the winner would take the set 5–3, for example. And a tie-break would mean it ended at 6–5, instead of 7–6). The standard tie-break would kick in at 5–5. Everything else in the set looks the same. As for the match format, it is the best of four sets, but the first to three. If nobody hits three and it ends up at 2–2 (of the shorter version set), a final-set tie-break to 10 will be played.

The longer format would make matches incredibly hard to win, adding the dimension to women's tennis that the men's side of things has. You could, effectively, still come back from 2–0 down. The matches would be longer, but not too long; they'd be more demanding – dramatic even – than the other tournaments, they would still differentiate in format from the men's five sets (and be less physically challenging, though more for the ladies), and they would have an additional entertainment factor that some have said has been missing at times when a lead of two sets to love wins all too frequently.

It solves the puzzle of the women playing identical matches to those in every other event in the year, hence elevating the Grand Slam tournaments to a new plain both physically and mentally, as well as offering a more dynamic spectacle for fans. It acknowledges that women are designed differently to men and should not be compared with the men or asked to play five sets of the same format as their male counterparts do. It recognises that Grand Slams demand something more beyond the seven match wins required to claim the grand prize. It evolves the women's game, perhaps drawing more fans to it, as the dynamic shift of best-of-four-and-a-half sets (essentially) offers more than three sets. The sets are a little shorter, meaning a maximum length match of four sets and a deciding tie-break to 10 would not last as long as a men's five-set match. Put simply, this scenario brings to life a match opportunity that is a halfway home between three and five sets. If I had to tamper with anything, it would be that. It would open up a new dimension and pose a new and greater physical and mental challenge.

Federer Fever

Near empty stands don't sum up how grandiose and special it is to see Roger Federer take to a tennis court again. The smattering of a crowd makes more than enough pro-Federer noise in the Doha Qatar Open second round, as one might expect.

The Federer–Evans tussle is epic. For a three-set match it is incredibly entertaining, back and forth, the pendulum swinging endlessly between the two men as they both find some of their best tennis. Federer is like a radio being tuned in to a channel. Having not been on court in some time, he would find the station, it would emit sound and words clearly, and then suddenly lose the channel. He clung on well at times, failing to reach his well-known heights, as one might imagine after 14 months off the tour, and there are glimpses of utter majesty (as one expects to always be near the maestro's game). Evans forces a deciding set after Federer had taken the lead in an incredibly close opener, with each man looking capable of claiming the victory today as the end approaches.

Federer's timing is, of course, not quite what we have come to expect from him on every point and every shot, but, By Jove, it is good to see him at it, plying his trade once again. Some shots are flashbacks of his best tennis over the years, spectators leaning in as the match drives towards its ending, but it's clear he's a little rusty, as anyone would be in his predicament. After 400 days without match play, Roger's comeback is a grand success.

This pair were recent practice partners and Dan Evans played his part today. He lit up the court at times with his own magic in a match that was anything but one-way traffic. Federer's brilliance came out, as did Evans's.

Evans attempted to rewrite the script but was foiled near the end as he tried to serve his way into a final-set tie-break and a chance of a shock that many did not want to witness. Federer wins 7–6, 3–6, 7–5. With more than a glimpse of the Swiss man's miracle tennis, it is a good starting point upon which to build, with lots to work on and many positives for both Federer and his team. The comeback everyone has been waiting for has already gathered a nice little head of steam.

He would go on to lose the following day to an in-form Nikoloz Basilashvili, who would claim the title by the end of the week, making it not seem such a bad loss as it did at the time.

Further del Potro Knee Surgery

Juan Martín del Potro has won one Grand Slam. He may well be unlikely now to add to that tally, but it's hard to argue that if he had been fit and not had a career hampered by serious injuries (he is presently fighting another one requiring a fourth surgery on his right knee) that the Big Three's own tally of majors would not quite look the way it presently does. Argentine del Potro has been one of the unlucky ones, no doubt. He has had it all – and many hope he will again – the big game, the ability to shatter the legends both physically and mentally, and take some scalps that, in doing so, were classic matches, reminding everyone of just what a special man he is on his day. The Tower of Tandil is working on a fresh comeback. Anyone who would not wish to see him in fine fettle and striking that ball as only he does is not a true fan of tennis, and perhaps only an admirer of individual greats and their quest to improve on their existing records.

Del Potro is a humble and compelling force on a tennis court. While never quite hitting the heights on clay, he has been at times extraordinary to watch on hard and grass courts. There were moments when it appeared a tennis ball could not be hit as powerfully and beautifully as this man struck it. His talent, his hitting, was, and will hopefully be again, beguiling, spell-like, addictive to watch. Forget who has won how many Grand Slams for a moment and consider that few have been, at their best, as fun, and admirable to watch as Juan Martín.

Remember the way he stole another US Open crown from Federer's head back in 2009 when he was a mere gangly 19-year-old. That those classic and epic scenes have never been repeated for del Potro on the biggest stages is a minor tragedy for the sport.

19 APRIL 2021

The On-Court Self Is the Real Self

There is no hiding what you are. The truth will out. You are not that good an actress/actor.

Everything you do on court shows what kind of a person you are. This is a remarkably fascinating sport for psychologists to observe closely, some of the animal and other behavioural patterns making them targets as though they were creatures under David Attenborough's nature programmes' lens.

Do you hurry the ball kids with less than elegance and understanding? Do you take longer than the allotted time for breaks, do you push and bend rules which – some of – have been in place for decades? Do you respect all opponents and your surroundings, those who make these events and your life possible?

Uncle Toni in Felix's Corner

A prize fighter has a world-class trainer in his or her corner. You had better believe that. No single great puts it all together in solitary fashion and sees all the ensuing success without greatly knowledgeable tacticians, coaches, fitness experts, and so on.

Félix Auger-Aliassime adding the legendary Toni Nadal – Rafa's famous Uncle Toni – to his team may prove a masterstroke and does indeed come as something of a bolt out of the blue. It's no secret that Félix has been training at Rafa's academy in Majorca, nor that the Canadian and the Spanish 20-time major winner get on very well and have a general approach and respect for the game in common. For every Kyrgios, the game needs a player with an attitude like Félix. It creates a balance within the sport, the yin and yang, the left and right, the traditions upheld versus the flamboyant tearing up of the rulebook.

The game is beautiful. Sometimes the spectacle is too much. Uncle Toni, in Félix's corner, gives a good young guy a shot at the big time that he might not have quite been lined up for before. If the talent is there for major titles, it's sure to be visible very soon under the tutelage of an absolute king of the coaching side of tennis.

Monte Carlo Masters 1000 Report

Evans Beats Djokovic in Pair's First Meeting

Monte Carlo has seen its first shock. Dan Evans, Great Britain's top-ranked player these days is, on his day, a ruthless opponent who can sink the ship of many a tennis player. He is heading back up towards the ranking he reached last time around – pre-drug ban period – when he was certainly a player many would not want to face in the early rounds. Known for being confrontational in game style and more, Evans made Djokovic look very average indeed, a feat few have managed, even in a period of well over a decade. Evans defeated Djokovic in two straight sets 6–4, 7–5 to lead their head-to-head 1–0.

Two Tight Singles Matches End the Day

Andrey Rublev versus Roberto Bautista Agut and Casper Ruud against Pablo Carreño Busta did not fail to deliver. The two matches played out at the same time and certainly echoing each other more than just a little were colossal battles that saw Rublev and Ruud conquer respectively. The last 16 was when seeds collided and, while the unseeded Ruud faced the higher-ranked Spaniard, both matches were of a truly high calibre throughout and signalled players hitting their strides when it most mattered to overcome tough opposition. Both matches were three-set encounters with tight patterns and the pendulum swinging, each player there, present, giving himself a chance.

The empty stands of Monte Carlo look somehow more tragic than many other venues. John Lennon once asked the people in the expensive seats to rattle their jewellery, and Monte Carlo feels like it is missing that punch of wealth and luxury the crowds bring annually.

Quarter-final Day

Casper Ruud v Fabio Fognini (defending champion here as there was no event in 2020) comes after Dan Evans has squeezed past David Goffin into the last four of a Masters for the first time. Stefanos Tsitsipas has advanced having played only one set, with Alejandro Davidovich Fokina retiring injured after losing a close first set with the Greek.

The winner of Ruud and Fognini will play the victor of today's last quarter-final following straight on from this, which is between Andrey Rublev and Rafael Nadal, the 11-time champion in Monte Carlo.

Rafa Eyes Number 12 and Falls Short

Messing with the seedings, Casper Ruud (who loves the clay), had come through his Italian test in the shape of defending champion Fabio Fognini. That was nothing compared with the legend of these courts that is Spaniard Nadal being shown the quarter-final exit door by Russian Rublev in a three-set match that definitely depicted Rublev as a clay court threat as he comfortably won the decider, tossing Nadal to the wolves, showing him he is far from the walk-in-the-park tennis that has seen many – including Rublev in his on-court interview post-previous round victory – running scared, not overly hopeful of knocking him off his perch.

Rublev won the first set, and a second set of gladiators lasting 1 hour and 13 minutes ensued, consisting of one epic game after another, many possible breaks, Nadal almost going 4–1 down, staying within reach, levelling at 4–4, holding and breaking serve to take a set that looked so unlikely a little time earlier. That is the man we have all come to know on clay, someone who never gives up. It's undeniable that these are two of the biggest hitters presently in the men's game.

The match takes 2 hours and 32 minutes. Rublev beats Nadal. Is the Spaniard done on clay? Is it this year? It's too early to tell, but it is perhaps on the cards as we witness the younger players now stampeding into the upper echelons of the game. I would not write Nadal's clay court playing obituary just yet. He lost here to eventual champion Fognini at the semi-final stage two years ago and has won the Roland Garros title twice since then. It's the first big clay court tournament of the season and provides an opportunity to brush up on one's skills on the clay again. It doesn't always reflect what will come later (despite Rafa having won it 11 times in the past, mostly going on to replicate that success in the imminent Parisian major). Nadal will certainly feel that the massive power and physical presence of Rublev could well prove a problem for him later in the clay court season, and Nadal has a way to go to reach his imperious best, though he does tend to find that in time for the French Open. If he is still able to do it, we will be witnessing it again over the next two months.

A First Time Masters Champion Will Be Crowned

The Monte Carlo Masters 1000 title will be the first of the level for one of either Andrey Rublev or Stefanos Tsitsipas. The two have been slowly improving over a number of years – Rublev stalled by a substantial back injury delay in 2018 – and now a golden opportunity for 1,000 points and a first Masters title is only hours away.

While the recent Hurkacz victory was made a little easier by the Big Three all being absent from the start, these two have overcome a field that included two of those three greats – Djokovic losing his first match of the year to Dan Evans, who was conquered earlier today by the Greek, Tsitsipas, with some ease. Rublev has himself completed the rather tough ask of removing Nadal from the draw in a very physical battle, only a day after taking around three hours to despatch of another Spaniard in Roberto Bautista Agut, and today beating ever-improving Norwegian Casper Ruud in two straight sets.

Everything is set up wonderfully for two players who were NextGen not so long ago, and with each passing event they become more a staple part of the top 10 and soon both the top five. It's hard to argue against Rublev being the most consistent and second-best player in the world behind Djokovic going into the final, regardless of present ranking (obviously distorted and misleading because of the frozen rankings, designed to protect players because of the pandemic and how it affected tennis through 2020).

Tsitsipas Gets There First

Of the two men, it was hard to predict who would emerge triumphant beforehand. The pair shared a head-to-head record of 3–3, both men had reached the final in impressive form, and on any given day anything could happen. Except a draw.

Tsitsipas started by far the better and didn't look back, building a beguiling head of steam, finally looking ready for his first Masters title, a natural step up from his other career wins (barring his biggest so far, the ATP Finals win in late 2019).

It looks to be the case of Rublev's batteries having run out and Tsitsipas being fresher and better from the outset. If both men found their best tennis at the same time, the outcome would inevitably have been a closer affair than the 6–3, 6–3 scoreline of their seventh professional career meeting.

Serbian Open Surprise

The Serbian Open in Belgrade may only be an ATP 250 event, and it might have worn the impression that the trophy would easily be collected by native Serbian and world number one Novak Djokovic, but there is always a player who has other ideas, regardless of whether they can successfully execute them or not.

The pair had met once before – at Djokovic's key career stamping ground of the Australian Open in Melbourne (only months earlier) – but that meant nothing on this occasion, as the year's surprise, Aslan Karatsev, forced a lengthy encounter with the home favourite and not only put a good show on but came out the winner, making their head-to-head 1–1.

In 3 hours and 25 minutes, Karatsev goes a little way to making amends for that loss to Novak in the semi-finals of the 2021 Australian major. Today, he out-Djokovic-ed the great himself. He knocked the Serbian off his local perch with all those adoring folks close by, and he didn't even celebrate the match come the final point's passing. Phenomenal scenes. Karatsev was 253 in the world rankings this time last year, and now he is flying towards the upper echelons now, backing up his start to the year. He would go on to lose the final to Berrettini, but somehow it wouldn't feel like he lost anything here, only that, once again, he has proven what a remarkable force he is to be reckoned with.

It was the longest ATP match of the year so far and Karatsev saved 23 break points – yes, TWENTY-THREE – against the world's highest ranked player. He beats the top seed and shocks many locals and tennis fans beyond. It feels like a good day for tennis.

Pressure on Rafa

The pressure is mounting. It's astonishing to think how he might successfully manage to shrug it off every year. Rafael Nadal knows match and tournament wins on clay like nobody else does. What he has built over the years also means an unprecedented burden to succeed. How might that feel, to have the weight of everyone's expectations on your shoulders? Anything less than victory being failure.

You wonder how the mental and physical strain of the clay court season and the weight of history on his shoulders is not too much. Time and time again he takes it all in his stride. Now, 16 years on from his first victory in Roland Garros, he alluded to the desire to improve, to find his best and most perfect clay court tennis, a perfectionist never really satisfied. An artist admiring his work, always with the feeling it could yet be improved, even if time is running out. This characteristic is what sets him apart from the field.

The rest of the field is visibly better this year, and it feels like the pressure to hold back time and keep everyone at bay gets bigger and harder with every passing year. Nadal will turn 35 during this year's French Open.

Twenty-one in 2021? Dare to dream? Or the pressure or somebody else's brilliance will finally tell?

Nadal improves his head-to-head over the Greek top-tenner Stefanos Tsitsipas to 7–2 with a stunningly sweet victory in the Barcelona Open final (6–4, 6–7, 7–5), one to truly savour.

Stuttgart Report

The Stuttgart draw is rather fetching with many top players attending, not to win a Porsche, I imagine (though what do I know), but rather to find some early clay court season form and build some momentum upon which to head towards the second Grand Slam of the year. The events come thick and fast now as we hurtle towards Roland Garros and the short grass court season beyond.

Mostly, the players that might be expected to prevail do so, and the quarter-finals see top seed Ashleigh Barty against Karolína Plíšková, Elina Svitolina play Petra Kvitová, Aryna Sabalenka face Anett Kontaveit, and Ekaterina Alexandrova opposing Simona Halep.

The silence of the crowd-less affair is exacerbated in the indoors arena of Stuttgart. It's as though you could hear a pin drop. Every single sound, in addition to the two players, their movements across the clay, the umpire shifting in her or his chair, and the ball kids scurrying, is picked up, amplified, echoing the absence of fans.

On semi-final day Saturday, Ashleigh Barty, 25 today, puts in a huge performance overturning a one-set deficit to beat Svitolina in three. With Svitolina having led 4–1 in the second set and letting the lead slip, Barty finally levelled the match via the tie-break. In the final set, Barty soon took the lead and didn't look back, comfortable in the end.

In the other last-four match, Sabalenka and Halep locked horns and Sabalenka prevailed in two relatively straightforward sets, 6–3, 6–2, showing her prowess once again on the bigger stage and that she has solidified her place in the world's top 10 and, with her best tennis, even has a chance of continuing to climb, perhaps even with the pinnacle in sight.

It has been a splendid week of tennis and the top players, as one might imagine, are looking focused and on a mission as they hurtle towards another Roland Garros.

The final pits Sabalenka, the number five seed, against the world number one and top seed, Barty. The silent indoors clay arena with three Porsches on show is an unusual affair. The occasional clap of a coach pricks the otherwise quiet match, with the sound of something faintly rustling as the contest advances, a few sounds reminding us it isn't a dream but the present reality. Sabalenka looks fearless, less overwhelmed by the bigger occasions than once she appeared. Barty hangs with her until 3–4 and then loses her serve with a failed drop shot. Barty loses the first set 3–6. She then whips up a storm and overpowers and blows away Sabalenka to lead 3–1 in the final set after giving Sabalenka a bagel in the second set. Sabalenka then breaks back to trail 2–3, back on serve. It then becomes a tug of war as Barty breaks to lead by two games again. Barty faces break points when serving to consolidate the break and is only a game away from the title. Barty gets to 5–2, holding firm. And it's the last chance for Sabalenka, who holds serve and then succumbs 6–3 in the final set.

Once again, Barty has proven her problem-solving skills to be as good as anyone's in the game, turning everything after the first set on its head and only losing another three games thereafter. Barty, heading deeper into the clay court season, looks very much the one to beat. Whether she can imminently replicate her 2019 Roland Garros – and first major – title win remains to be seen. Sabalenka takes the defeat badly and hurls her racket towards her bench beside the court before reclaiming it to tap rackets at the net with Barty. You cannot help but feel such blatant outbursts might just be where her age and her weaknesses bring her down. Barty, calm as you like, is seldom fazed and works out what needs doing to end up on the winning side of the net. While it might be inherent to her character, it certainly lends to a title-winning package.

Lost Rybakina Rhythm

Doubtlessly – Elena Rybakina is not the only player – the pandemic arrived and threw the routine tennis players knew well out of the window. Some stayed at home, some made decisions based on the location of events and the situation of the pandemic at that time there, and others continued as normal, with all kinds of responses and coping mechanisms keeping them rolling or hurting.

Few players, however, could claim to have been in the kind of form and run that Rybakina was when tennis was – as many other things were – shut down.

Resuming, restarting the engine is not easy after such a lengthy time-out, as with an injury, and while still very young with years ahead of her, we will now never know what could have come of the form she was in.

Lots of questions will remain unanswered, though as with anything in life, how we respond to adversity and bounce back when it is possible might also define us.

At a Stretch

Ashleigh Barty and Aryna Sabalenka are becoming something of a familiar match-up; Barty, with her relaxed manner and Sabalenka stretching to find it all within her capacity, close at hand, to find the tennis that she believes can undo Barty. They played two weeks ago in Stuttgart, Sabalenka winning the opening set and then Barty finding her magical recipe to win in three. This was an immediate chance at redemption for Sabalenka, as well as to stop the rot of Barty having won the last two contests between the pair on the bounce. If the Belarusian wins today, it would make their head-to-head 4–4.

Sabalenka looks pushed, Barty laid back. Sabalenka takes a 2–0 lead though, breaking Barty after a close first service game for the world number one. Sabalenka is in no mood to mess around as she holds serve again and proceeds to break Barty to 30 for a 4–0 lead. There's a long way to go, but Sabalenka doesn't care what happened recently – if anything, it is simply further motivation to do what she knows she can. What a start from Sabalenka, whose aggressive game plan has thus far been expertly executed.

And … somewhat unpredictably, Sabalenka wins the first set 6–0 – a becoming bagel on the score board – in 25 minutes.

But one set does not win a match, and Barty is soon on the score board and with a break of her own up at 2–0 in the second. Sabalenka gets it back to 2–2 with her fourth break of the Barty serve today.

Barty is, as ever, cool, calm, and collected, and 4–2 up, edging in front well. That lead becomes 5–3 and she breaks Sabalenka, really frustrating her opponent, to level the match at one set all and force a decider. 0–6, 6–3 reads the scoreboard.

When Barty holds early in the deciding set of a now compelling ladies final in Madrid, it is the first time she has led in the match. With every point that fails to go her way you can see Sabalenka losing her composure. Is this where Barty undoes her slightly younger opponent? Barty backs herself to win the match, even when handed a bagel set, never questioning her powers. Sabalenka is having a meltdown now as she feels it all slipping from her reach. It has been coming. The meltdown – and this is where it is key – is more than visible, as she carries the spectators with her as she implodes. The Belarusian is increasingly aggressive, motioning with her racket, and in her general body language. She is showing Barty that the Australian has her right where she wants her, mentally flailing. Sabalenka manages to hang on though, at 1–2, and levels things up. With so much on the line, she may need to channel her frustrations or say goodbye to the title for this year. Soon it is 4–3, still on serve, Barty with the edge that comes with serving first.

Then, at 4–4, Barty suddenly capitulates and is broken to love. It comes out of nowhere and stops the pattern the set had previously followed as it edged ever closer towards a deciding set tie-break.

Sabalenka serves for the title and makes no mistake. A brilliant win, especially after losing the second set and a wobble early in the decider. You can't help but hope they meet in the French Open final next month. This – right now, and on clay – is the best match-up of the ladies' game.

Surprise Final

The somewhat surprising final of Alexander Zverev – past winner of the Madrid Open in 2018 – and Matteo Berrettini provides the Spanish capital with a breath of fresh air and another non-Big Three showpiece match.

Berrettini, perhaps causing some eyebrows to raise, takes first blood by breaking in game seven. He then goes down 0–30 in his next service game. It is soon 15–40 and two immediate break-back points to the German. The predictable return to parity follows and a tie-break is called for. Berrettini is 5–0 up. That becomes 6–4. And somehow 6–6, meaning a less than likely change of ends at the last change is needed with the tie-break still not falling into one player's lap. The Italian, eventually, finds a way to win it 10–8 with Zverev making a crucial double fault before a huge Berrettini serve that cannot be returned over the net.

While others might crumble, the tie-break loss is just what Zverev needs to catalyse him into conjuring some of his best tennis.

As the second set goes with serve, Berrettini saving break points at 3–3, the set careens towards a tie-break again. Zverev, however, has different ideas, and finally seizes and yanks the reins, and pulls off the necessary break and takes it 6–4, pushing a final set.

The last time the first three Masters winners of the year were all new was 1990. They were Stefan Edberg, Pete Sampras, and Andrei Chesnekov. This year so far, we have had two first-timers with Hubert Hurkacz (Miami) and Stefanos Tsitsipas (Monte Carlo). If Berrettini takes this last set, the same will have happened again, 31 years later.

Zverev uses all his experience, pulls it off 6–3 in the decider, subjects Berrettini to the runner-up spot, and claims his second Madrid title and his fourth overall Masters win. The Masters titles have become a little less predictable in recent times as the Big Three invariably eye the majors more than anything else.

21 ROME OPEN 2021

Serena Playing Is Always a Big Day

The occasion is more than just Serena's return to competitive action for the first time since 18th February when she lost in the Australian Open semi-final to Naomi Osaka – it is her 1,000th career match. How many players will ever get that far?

While obviously rusty after so long away again, Serena brings a commitment and desire to the court that is not the case for many players. That she is still hungry for more is perhaps extraordinary, though if we didn't know this about her by now, we never will. Her reputation and sterling success precede her, but she knows that isn't enough to carry her to any future victory. Nadia Podoroska isn't overwhelmed and soon breaks Serena to take an early 2–1 lead in the first set of the pair's Italian Open second-round match.

Serena fires back excellently, immediately reclaiming parity and showing she will be anything but a pushover regardless of her recent absence from professional competition. She often finds her groove frighteningly quickly again, in fact.

Things remain level until Podoroska breaks for 5–4, and again when serving to consolidate – only this time to win the set – she is broken. 5–5. Crowd or no crowd, things are heating up nicely.

Last year's Roland Garros semi-finalist Podoroska is Serena's match today, and in two tight sets ensures not being pushed to a final set, winning 7–6, 7–5. Much room for improvement for the legendary American, but will she get enough matches in before the French capital calls? The question is, when she can quickly find such a high level anyway, how much is it damaging her chances of that twenty-fourth Grand Slam success when she tends to play so few events prior to those majors? If she looks around, all the players in form at each major have been playing for months on the surface before the major tournaments. On the face of it, she starts every major with a distinct disadvantage, however superior she has been and may even continue to be. Given time's relentless ticking, she could do with giving herself the absolute best possible chance for that long sought-after record-equalling major title.

It was a big day. On this occasion it was not to be. Who knows what comes next?

Big First Meeting

Grand Slam-winning teenager (imminently turning 20 years of age), Iga Świątek, currently ranked 15 and heading at light speed for the top 10 of the game, faces past world number one Karolína Plíšková in the pair's first ever meeting in today's Italian Open final. Taking place in a WTA 1000 event is reason to be pumped, but with so much at stake going into the year's second major this could well be the final building block that puts one of these women on a pedestal that others would love to knock them off at the coming Roland Garros in two weeks' time.

Świątek serves first and flies out of the blocks winning the game to love, showing what she is about very succinctly. Plíšková's ship has been steadied, after some poor results in recent years, by the addition to her team of coach Sascha Bajin (on board with Naomi Osaka in her early major triumphs, having worked with Kristina Mladenovic and Dayana Yastremska in between).

Świątek is wide awake and pouncing on anything, very early into her groove, fashioning a break point immediately that she snaps up to lead

2–0 over her far more experienced opponent. Four points later, Świątek is halfway to the first set without having lost a point on her serve yet; a brutal young force sweeping through another clay court tournament as if she had forgotten her age and relative lack of experience, converting quiet confidence into match scenarios to slip under her belt and arm her in future encounters.

Plíšková launches an assault of double faults and sets herself back further, soon behind 4–0. The extraordinary one-sidedness of the final continues as Świątek obliterates everything Plíšková gives her and takes the set 6–0 in a mere 20 minutes (it still says 0:19 when the set ends, but later it will show the time of 0:22). That is a bagel that must seriously hurt Plíšková, who has not even got her engine started yet, thus far winning only four points.

Świątek is not only a huge Rafa fan but more than a little resembles her Spanish hero devouring another opponent on the red European clay that must also provide a nightmare backdrop for many others. As Plíšková slips 15–40 down and double faults to hand a 6–0, 2–0 lead to her younger opponent, it looks like it might be one of the most one-sided finals in memory. The demolition takes a rest, and Plíšková finally gets two break points and sees a glimmer of light but, as with great players, the danger is quickly extinguished by Świątek, and the demolition continues. The double faults keep adding up as the pressure on Plíšková's shoulders visibly mounts, and it is a shocking scene of a tennis match. Plíšková cannot solve the puzzle, cannot get anywhere near Świątek's level, and it all looks too easy, over in three quarters of an hour with the scoreline of 6–0, 6–0 (a double bagel). Plíšková has had her deficiencies laid out in front of her, trampled on, and shown to the rest of the global tennis community. It is a total humiliation and surely makes Świątek a strong favourite for Paris. You can only beat the player put in front of you. For Iga Świątek, it is a job perfectly done, and this match will go down with the most one-sided finals in the history of tennis. For the loser, it is a hard outcome to swallow, leaving some folk speechless.

This first meeting will give Plíšková nightmares for a long time. Not the sensation you want to take with you into an imminent major tournament, not at all.

If the word 'wow' is not on your lips for one reason or another at the end of this match, it never will be.

- The match is over in three quarters of an hour (sets of 22 and 23 minutes on the official WTA match clock).
- The total points distribution is 51 for Świątek, 13 for Plíšková.
- Six out of eight break points won for Świątek, zero out of two for Plíšková.
- Plíšková six double faults, her opponent made none.

Clash of the Titans

While the Roger Federer–Rafael Nadal rivalry may be the one people are fondest of, the one between Novak Djokovic and Nadal is unarguably the greatest and the one with the deepest well of brilliance. Today, the two men meet for the fifty-seventh time. They have played each other in every year since 2006, and the split is almost even at 29 wins for Djokovic and 27 for Nadal. It has been, and somehow continues to be, an extraordinary show over 15 years of elite action that has left others dumbfounded.

With the greatest men's rivalry in modern tennis, history is on the line once more. If Nadal wins, he joins level with Djokovic again as the leader of most Masters titles won (36). If Djokovic wins, daylight, the lead up to two (37–35).

You can almost hear the other – all much younger – players (the ones left in their wake in a trail of destruction this week: Stefanos Tsitsipas, Alexander Zverev, Denis Shapovalov, Jannik Sinner, Lorenzo Sonego, Reilly Opelka, Alejandro Davidovich Fokina, and Taylor Fritz), their words echoing still days later as they discussed their encounters with the legends with their teams. The question on their lips would all be the same – HOW are they doing THIS? How are they keeping alive and holding back the hands of time? How do they keep shutting us out as we get fitter and stronger and better at what we do? Should they not have been consigned to the shadows by now? What more can we do?

Both men come into this final having clung on for dear life with the type of tennis that has made them each so legendary. We could be in for a thriller here.

A mini battle of almost nine minutes takes place in game two and Djokovic goes up an early break. Rafa will not panic, but it looks in the first moments like this is peak clay court Djokovic, which means Nadal is in for a tough one today. The Spaniard, however, gets his teeth into his nemesis in the next game and breaks back to get his first game and placate the excited scoreboard. It is soon 2–2 and Nadal has settled into the match, having gauged the measure of his opponent's electric start.

Things continue as normal until the seventh game with an exchange of easier service games. Nadal gets a break point, but Djokovic finds his most masterful shots at the key moment and, after a lengthy tussle, a Nadal fall, post-astonishing-winner, and the usual mounting of tension, Djokovic emerges 4–3 up. A thrilling and awfully close first set finally finishes after 75 minutes when Nadal breaks for 6–5 and then successfully serves it out, having been down 15–30 on serve.

In set two, a Nadal dip equals a Djokovic peak, and in less than half an hour of the inevitably middle set of the match the Serb is 4–1 up. Nadal then has another tough service game, and again Djokovic has all the answers and finally forces his way through the door to a double break. He leads 5–1 and will serve to level the match at one set all. When Djokovic does indeed pocket the set 6–1, it begs the question of what has happened to Nadal for him to plummet so quickly from the heights of the first set and the accompanying euphoria.

A one-set shoot-out coming right this way. Nadal crackles with his unparalleled electrical current early in the decider and threatens the Serb's serve. But Djokovic's response wave is remarkable and takes over for an interlude. Nadal is in danger in game five, and the match hangs in the balance as the incredible tension in the arena fills every corner and beyond, spilling out of television screens all over the globe – the anticipation before the match being fulfilled. Nadal stays ahead, though it is not easy to see how. Djokovic failing to covert his chance is a burden in the next game and he shows Nadal three break points. Nadal loves the invitation and snaps up the very first, breaking to love, and having won the last seven points in a row to surge ahead in a set that had looked to be going the other way. Can he consolidate that important break of serve? Nadal is two games from the title. He does push the right buttons and reaches 5–2. It's hard to see how Djokovic can now claw his way back, though never say never, and if the past has taught us anything, it is that if anyone can it is this Serbian fellow. What an encounter – while not their most classic of matches – this has again proven to be.

They are never done, this pair. It feels like the rivalry to end them all for competitiveness and sheer brute force and will. We will perhaps never see anything even remotely like this again. To think we have Roger returning soon is almost too much excitement to take. Let's continue to enjoy this era while we are still living in it, for soon it will be a remarkable thing of the past, history awaiting the three men.

Djokovic serves at 2–5 to stay in the final and keep his chances of a turnaround alive. Djokovic is in trouble and faces match point. He manages to wriggle free from the shackles to hold serve. 5–3. Over to Nadal ... who does indeed win his tenth title in Rome. It is his thirty-sixth Masters title, as he draws level with Djokovic on that figure. His career total of titles is now up to 88. The head-to-head is still led by Djokovic but has been cut to 29–28 in his favour.

With 2:49 on the match clock, Nadal wins 7–5, 1–6, 6–3. Nadal with 37 winners, 26 on the forehand side. He becomes the oldest winner of the Italian Open – at almost 35 years of age.

22 SUMMER IS COMING

Serena and Roger

At similar times on Tuesday, 18th May 2021, Roger Federer and Serena Williams lose first sets in their respective tennis matches – second round encounters of tournaments in Geneva, Switzerland (men's) and Parma, Italy (women's).

However, where Serena loses her second set against Kateřina Siniaková by a much greater margin than their close first set (Serena succumbing 7–6, 6–2), Roger turns the 4–6 tables to get the second by that same scoreline over Pablo Andújar in the pair's first ever meeting.

It's hard to know what is left in the Serena tank, both mentally and physically. She has been a revelation over more than two decades. Regardless of the losses at the four Grand Slam finals in which she had bid to win a twenty-fourth and record-equalling major title (to draw level with Margaret Court, a player from a wholly different time, era, mindset, and physicality of the game), since returning from giving birth she has done very little to earn less than the utmost respect for how she has strived for and hit incredible heights. While not attaining the holy grail of that elusive title, she has shown everyone what a mother, a warrior, and a remarkable talent can achieve. The French Open awaits, and who knows what lurks around the corner for Serena. Either way, she has nothing left to prove.

As Federer takes it to a final set and then breaks early on, things appear to be on course for the victory everyone – well, almost – wants to see. But Andújar, wearing shades of the pantomime villain of the piece, has other ideas, and breaks back for 4–4 and holds serve to put all the pressure back on the Swiss man's shoulders. Roger will serve to stay in the match. Is he to follow Serena out the 'exit' door, also failing to get the desired matches under the belt before Paris?

At 15–40, Roger hits an incredible backhand winner to stay in it a moment more. Federer then brings his most incisive game to get to deuce, everyone on tenterhooks. He mishits and faces another match point, and this time loses the point, and thereby the match. From 4–2 up in the final set, Roger has lost the match. It's not what many wanted and leaves a question mark over his imminent Parisian possibilities, especially considering that Grand Slam men's tennis is best-of-five.

Andújar, though, with a brilliant performance, has his moment in the spotlight. He said before the match that he had played Rafa (he trails their head-to-head by 4–0), and Novak (2–0 down in their head-to-head), and that he had always wanted to collect and savour the experience of a career meeting with Roger to be able to tell his kids and grandkids about one day. He now has a victory to tell them all about to boot.

And so now, yes, at 35 (Andújar) and 39 (Federer) years of age, the pair have played their first match, and Andújar walks away, for now, leading his head-to-head over one of the two greatest players ever to live (or at least based on current Grand Slam tallies).

Halep Roland Garros Withdrawal a Huge Blow

The first major blow has been dealt to Roland Garros before it even kicks off. Simona Halep, the 2018 champion, has pulled out owing to the recent injury sustained at the Italian Open in Rome. Halep has often been there or thereabouts at the French Open in recent years. While her form going into it might not have seen her best clay court season, well, she can never be counted out, and it is one brilliant player fewer for the other main contenders to deal with.

You cannot help but feel it is a loss, because Halep has been central to some brilliant matches over the best part of a decade now and is always good value at the major tournaments. Hopefully, her injury won't be an issue for long and she can finally defend her Wimbledon 2019 title – two years on – as the year's third major finally takes place again in 2021.

Casper Ruud Shines

Norwegian third seed Casper Ruud is a match for most players on clay. Today bears witness to the claiming of the second ATP title of his career – the Gonet Geneva Open – and he looks very good against the slightly higher-ranked second seed Canadian Denis Shapovalov, himself looking to crack the top 10 soon.

Ruud has proven over the course of the entire clay court season that he is one of the main men to beat, a red dirt force to be reckoned with. He outshines Shapovalov and will be a threat to anybody in Paris when this year's second major gets underway.

The win puts Ruud back into the top 20 in the ATP rankings. He is one to watch in the remainder of the year and beyond, and while there are many names of the younger generation that have been talked about much more, at still only 22, Ruud is looking to join those players as one for the next 10 years or so.

In his winner's speech, Ruud congratulated Denis and said he felt sorry for him on Thursday when he had to play two matches in one day. It's the first encounter of the pair's head-to-head. Having played in juniors and now initiated the professional career rivalry, this could be an interesting one going into the future. Regardless of today's outcome, both men are hotter than ever on the red European clay courts.

Casper Ruud is a tennis symbol of the power of understatement. Whether he catches everybody's eyes or not, as some players do, here is a player to follow in his quest. Much more to come from him.

Shapovalov can feel buoyed. He is becoming the player he showed he was capable of being five years ago when he first exploded onto the scene.

Tuning in to the French Open Frequency

The players have turned up, or at least done their best to do so as the clay run heads for its big showdown in Paris. The qualifying event has begun, and there's no denying now that it's one of the biggest tests of the season, the prize everyone is eyeing with great interest, to add another to a tally or breakthrough to the big time on one of the ultimate stages of the sport.

The breakneck speed with which we race through Paris and to the following grass court tournaments that lead into Wimbledon defines the annual early summer period but also aids its passing, almost too quickly, as familiarity both comforts and alienates us.

23 ROLAND GARROS 2021

The French Open as a TV Series

1. **An early rewrite to everybody's expectations is needed when Dominic Thiem becomes the first major casualty of the 2021 French Open. His recent lack of form has seen him ousted in a stunning comeback by Pablo Andújar (yes, he who put Roger Federer out in Geneva recently) from two 2–0 down.**

Before the event, the big news was that the Big Three – the oft-labelled GOATs of the game – had been drawn in the very same half of the men's draw. The Thiem result only adds to the early intrigue surrounding the tournament. It's a highlight to the opening episode of the series and once again – as if it was needed – reiterates how epic the best-of-five format truly is.

Episode one is mostly routine, laying the foundations for what is to come later. Some well-known players do not have it easy; others hit the cruise button and seamlessly end up in the next round.

There is a tantalising early encounter between Aryna Sabalenka and the returning-to-form Croatian Ana Konjuh. Sabalenka has matured a lot and should be a contender for the title here if she brings her best tennis-playing self to the event. She wins the match in two sets, 6–4, 6–3.

In one final piece of dream-like news, it is announced that in the ladies' doubles draw this year, Venus Williams and Cori Gauff will pair up.

2. We get a peek at some more splendid Iga Swiatek tennis, welcome Roger Federer back to Paris – and Grand Slam tennis – and, in the night session on the Philippe-Chatrier court, Serena Williams does what Serena Williams does best and gives us another hour and 42 minutes of vintage memories of her as she speeds towards her destiny once again over the coming month and a half.

Stealing the stage today, the Naomi Osaka saga reaches a potential conclusion for now when she withdraws from the tournament. It must be a new reason for departing a major tournament when still very much in its draw, though of this I cannot be certain. She states that for the sake of the tournament, the players, her own well-being, and not wanting to cause a distraction or take anything away from the event – thereby preserving her fragile mental health – it is better to withdraw. The fallout from her announcement last week of a media blackout and following it through yesterday meant that it would result in a war between one player and the four Grand Slams – not to mention the WTA. While it's a loss to any draw – regardless of whether she likes or is any good on clay or not – to see her fall by the wayside, it's the way it happens this time that feels disappointing for everyone. Of course, no one player is ever as big as a sport, but with communication, hard work, and understanding, everybody can perhaps find a more comfortable way – even under the spotlight – to coexist.

3. There is talk about Osaka's withdrawal, and mental health in tennis is under a spotlight as much as it ever has been. Everyone is swinging their opinion as if it were a racket, and there is even a little tennis. Well, as first rounds tend to have, plenty in fact, as the final matches of round one in the men's and women's singles take place.

Seventeen-year-old Océane Babel (a French force of the future) is beaten 6–2, 7–5 by the experienced head of Elina Svitolina.

Petra Kvitová withdraws with an injury sustained during her media requirements on Sunday – an unfortunate slip on a step that turned her ankle, and she is, unfortunately, the latest casualty to succumb and withdraw without any match play on a tennis court.

Late in the day, Sloane Stephens plays the villain (no reflection on the American) when all eyes are on her meeting with recent cancer survivor Carla Suárez Navarro. The Spaniard, in her first match since overcoming her illness, came incredibly close to winning a match that, in the end, just stretched her marginally too far. She will have enjoyed the moment, not the outcome, and has much to be remarkably proud of. Let's hope that before she hangs up her racket for good later this year we all have something of the old Carla to watch and celebrate, along with the wonderful and inspirational figure that she is.

As the series progresses, the sense of familiarity and inevitability is counterbalanced by the endless shocks, magic, and excitement for what is to come.

4. **As the second round commences, the plot thickens. There are stories within stories, subplots, and endless questions from all angles to be answered. If we had not already been sucked into the storyline, the reduction of 64 players in each the women's and the men's draw to 32 is enough to incite a deeper sense of exhilaration.**

Victoria Azárenka and Madison Keys set up a third-round match after conquering the two talented youngsters Clara Tauson and Leylah Fernandez respectively. Both straight-sets victories, and Tauson puts up a good fight in both sets, and Fernandez finds her way into the match in the second only to narrowly miss out in the final stages.

Paula Badosa continues to move through the gears of this clay court season (having won the Serbia Open only a week before Roland Garros kicked off as well as reaching the semi-finals in the Madrid Open in early May), a threat for the latter stages of this year's women's event. Badosa beats Danka Kovinić 6–2, 6–0, wasting absolutely no time on court.

Serena Williams is delayed in taking to the court by Karen Khachanov and Mr five-set Kei Nishikori taking their match all the way – the Japanese winning it – in a 3-hour-and-59-minute encounter that Nishikori had trailed in.

Serena eventually gets on court a couple of hours later and is pushed, this time by Romanian world number 174 Mihaela Buzărnescu (as high as 20 back in 2018 before the repeated curse of injuries claimed her, not to mention the pandemic, and stopped her from improving on that ranking). Buzărnescu craftily pockets the second set when it had looked like a tie-break would decide it. Serena made no mistake with the final set, winning it 6–1. She will face fellow countrywoman Danielle Collins in the next round. That could be a real scream-fest!

5. **The unexpected invites us further in as the plot twists and turns. Not just a tennis event, it is a microcosm of life and the tennis tours – everything we find attractive about the sport is on show here.**

The latest unfortunate shock – again in the ladies' event – is when one of the favourites Ashleigh Barty retires injured (an injury that has troubled her already this week) at 2–2 in the second set, and a set down, against Pole Magda Linette. This again robs the draw of a player who surely would have had something to say and likely progressed to the latter stages. We have, for one reason or another, already lost Simona Halep (pre-tournament), Naomi Osaka (controversial withdrawal), Petra Kvitová (unfortunate injury-related withdrawal), and now Barty, to add to the others who have fallen in the early stages. One woman is going to swoop in and take advantage.

Marin Čilić has won a Grand Slam and appeared in the final of several others. While clay is his least favoured surface, he is no pushover, and if he flexes his muscle on court Philippe-Chatrier – a task he pulls off best here in the second set – against Roger Federer today, still on the comeback trail, the Swiss may have a job on his hands. It's a great match, the pair's first meeting since that famous 2018 Australian Open final that Federer won in five sets (to claim his twentieth major). In the first set, Roger is sublime, taking it swiftly – as he does best – and perhaps surprising everyone, himself included, by six games to two.

If you have to play your way into form after such a lengthy delay as Federer had, then these kinds of matches are perfect for that. As he snatches the third set on a tie-break, after dropping the second, it looks like just the tune-up he needed. As his ship comes into harbour in four sets, it is only to admire how on earth he is still managing this. It's an outlier in sport that someone of his age – as perfectly made for the sport as he is – can continue at the level he is somehow managing now, even after so few matches. If Wimbledon was watching this, it will be quivering in its boots with excitement at the thought of Roger attending its imminent event and what might, just might happen there.

The dark horse on the women's side is certainly Cori Gauff who makes serene progress. It's a question of *when* and not *if* with her, and it would not be a shock if her major breakthrough was any minute now, despite her tender years. She is one of *those* players.

On Rafael Nadal's thirty-fifth birthday proceedings in France are as most other years, as he lodges a late-night win over Frenchman Richard Gasquet in the haunting silence (far from standard) of night-time court Philippe-Chatrier (in the battle of two of the sweatiest players).

Nadal is in full and glorious wrecking ball flow again, despatching one of the players he grew up playing as a teen. Nadal speeds – in a relatively fast 18 minutes for him – into a 4–0 lead. It is soon a bagel set (6–0) to the Spaniard.

Set two starts with 0:27 on the match clock. Can Gasquet find anything? It's a paltry showing so far, unfortunately. Philippe-Chatrier starts to feel like the setting for a horror show for watching French fans and anyone who doesn't want Nadal to claim a fourteenth title here. However, Gasquet does bring some of his best tennis to the silent party. Nadal had surged into a lead but was then surprisingly pegged back and at 5–5 things become increasingly complicated for the reigning champion. He then finds that special gear and claims the two games needed to take a two-set lead. Had Nadal taken his foot off the accelerator? It seems unlikely. The great unheard of.

Monsieur Gasquet should definitely take a bow as he has put up fierce resistance and demonstrated to everyone how beautiful his tennis can be (eventually losing 6–0, 7–5, 6–2). He played some great stuff, and the match got what it had been missing in the first set – a contest that was entertaining to watch – regardless of whether it had a crowd or not. Sad for Gasquet to have an empty-seated venue for a match against such a player as Nadal. How many more times will such a meeting be possible?

6. **Grand Slam tennis singles' tournaments are in seven acts. Act 3 commences today with the standard fireworks (some real ones nearby actually halt the Badosa–Bogdan match briefly later in the day) as well as straightforward victories.**

The early surprise of the day is that Aryna Sabalenka – the highest remaining seed in the ladies' draw at the start of the day – loses 6–4, 2–6, 6–0 in three sets to Anastasia Pavlyuchenkova, who herself has not gone past the round of 32 in Paris in a decade, the final set being surely one of the most peculiar bagels we will see at this tournament. Sabalenka, only weeks earlier, had shown her major winning credentials by solving the Barty puzzle in the final in Madrid (having lost to her only two weeks earlier). Now, she fails at the third hurdle against a player you cannot help but feel she would likely beat eight times out of 10 on an average day. A very strange scoreline to say the least and it beggars the questions, 'When will Sabalenka deliver on the Grand Slam stage?' She keeps climbing the rankings, barely anywhere else left to go up.

The Ruud v Davidovich Fokina match turns out to be a five-set thriller. Both men are red hot at stages and unable to handle the brilliance of their opponent at others, back and forth the pendulum goes, and not until the last point is won is it even remotely clear who will conquer. And will the victor, today Davidovich Fokina, have anything left in the tank for the coming days? This match was 4 hours and 35 minutes and has been *that* epic match of the first week.

It looks like Daniil Medvedev – who had never won a match in four previous visits to Roland Garros – has found the clay court match-winning recipe. He pounded the in-form Reilly Opelka in straight sets – 6–4, 6–2, 6–4. He has gone from having zero self-professed hope on clay to being a threat.

Elena Rybakina impressed again and will now face Serena Williams – who won the battle of the Americans over Danielle Collins – in the last 16. The Kazakh player beat Elena Vesnina in one easy set and one harder set, shining at times as she did in early 2020 before her run that started the year was curtailed by the pandemic. Victoria Azárenka continued to look very sharp as she easily cast aside Madison Keys and faces Pavlyuchenkova in the next round (with a potential last-eight encounter with Serena in the following round).

7. **The final places in the last 16 are sorted, the elite making themselves known. Some have not had a great clay court season, but this is what counts, this is when turning up means the most – the biggest prize is there, the biggest payday, the most eyes watching on, and the chance for fame and glory.**

Elina Svitolina goes the way of Aryna Sabalenka and exits. She is another player who just cannot convert her on-court successes from the WTA events to the Grand Slam stage.

If the winning of a slam – even just one, à la Carolina Wozniacki or Marin Čilić – separates one from the remainder of the talented tennis players, then failure to convert a high ranking and tournament victories at every other level doesn't go unnoticed and must deeply irk the players who have the ability but are found wanting elsewhere. Surely nobody would settle for that.

The increasingly impressive form of Barbora Krejčíková in the singles – perhaps inspired by her doubles major-winning success, Roland Garros 2018 to name one – continues, as she comfortably outplays world number six and fifth seed Svitolina in two sets. The ladies' seeds are dropping like flies, the draw looking a little more decimated with each passing day. Only Sofia Kenin (4), who would beat fellow countrywoman and twenty-eighth seed Jessica Pegula in three sets today, having dropped the opener, is left above Serena Williams (7) in the seedings.

This is easily Krejčíková's biggest singles victory to date and is the kind of win to draw attention to her.

Women's tennis continues to thrive, throwing surprise after surprise at fans of the sport. What next?

Rafael Nadal moves on, improving his record at the French Open to 103–2 when he beats Cameron Norrie in round three. Yep, barely possible to believe that stat.

The night session is an eerie and long-lasting affair. Roger Federer meets German Dominik Koepfer. They trade blows – there are 12 points in a row against the serve at the midway mark in the second set – and some surprising breaks and after 2 hours it is a set apiece, both having culminated in tie-breaks.

Roger battles hard, far from his best, against a determined and pumped player in Koepfer. Federer wins in around 3.5 hours, 7–6, 6–7, 7–6, 7–5, but at what cost. It is a gruelling encounter that might live to tell a tale of its own.

There is something tragic about watching the ageing Federer in an empty stadium swinging for dear life at either side of midnight in Paris. Even though he wins, it is one of the haunting moments of this year's tournament – night sessions during curfew being crowd-less scenarios that highlight the sometime loneliness of the tennis profession – and if he'd sustained a fresh injury in this hellish encounter, there would not have been many surprised onlookers.

8. **Expect the unexpected in the ladies' draw. Recent years have taught us that well, have they not? The story is starting to reveal its bones, the surprises now defining the event, magic emerging from the unlikeliest of corners.**

Fittingly, Tamara Zidanšek – world number 85 – becomes the first name into the last eight.

Anastasia Pavlyuchenkova v Victoria Azárenka is something of a break-fest and goes into a final set. It opens with two breaks of serve, Azárenka then gets a warning for a time violation before the first point of the third game has got going. It was all downhill from there as she succumbed 6–2 in the third and Pavlyuchenkova, deservedly so, matched her career best run at a major by booking her place in the Paris quarter-finals.

Elena Rybakina storms out of the blocks against Serena Williams with a hold that signals her intentions loud and clear. Rybakina is looking more and more the part.

Rybakina's hitting is glorious from the word 'go!' and Serena has no answer, and despite the American's legendary prowess and phenomenal list of accomplishments this is what we want to see – talented young players coming through who are not intimidated and have the answers by just playing their tennis and overpowering whoever is at the other end of the court. Rybakina is soon 4–1 up. The clean and precise shots of the younger of the pair, the Kazakh, have Serena in all kinds of trouble, showing where she is lacking, where in the past she was not. The first set is soon over, and Rybakina is only a set away from her biggest career win to date.

When Rybakina serves at 4–5 down in set two you fear for her, but she holds well, then spectacularly breaks to love, putting the match on her own racket. Four points. For a place in the quarter-finals and a huge step forward for her. She takes it in her stride and wins the match only moments later, entirely unfazed as she served for it. Respect for her opponent means she shows a small smile and moves to the net to shake hands with the legend of the game who, once again, has fallen short, despite the opportunity here. This is Rybakina's moment, and she has almost certainly arrived on the big stage.

Stefanos Tsitsipas and Daniil Medvedev both hugely impress in their fourth-round matches and find their ways into a last-eight meeting together in two days' time, beating their opponents in straight sets – Pablo Carreño Busta and Cristian Garín respectively.

Roger Federer has withdrawn today after last night's arduous late match win. Losing Serena and Roger on the same day might be a tragedy for some, but it also shows that the shift to the young players is well in progress now.

9. **Plenty of swinging and missing and hearts breaking as players fail to hit the heights and push on through to the last eight. Some come close, some are nowhere near, the men and women are separated from the boys and girls and, while there is much more to come, we are now getting down to the nitty-gritty of the story.** Barbora Krejčíková makes her massive breakthrough by beating past Grand Slam champion and one-time Roland Garros finalist Sloane Stephens to reach the quarter-finals. It is brutal and, while closer than the 6–2, 6–0 scoreline suggests, is also a little humiliating for a player of the reputation of Stephens, who has no answer on this occasion.

Coco Gauff is growing in stature with every passing match. She fears nobody and looks set for the big time. Gauff is ruthless and comfortably beats Ons Jabeur to reach the quarter-finals. She has pure hunger to win in her eyes, it decoratively adorns her headbanded visage.

Lorenzo Musetti – who has never lost a professional tie-break in six this year and two previous ones – wins the first two sets on tie-breaks for a remarkable and unlikely lead over Novak Djokovic. The match then becomes unrecognisable to its first two sets, though much more standard for the world number one, as it is all completely flipped over in less than an hour as Djokovic in all his predictable glory wins the third and fourth, breaks in the deciding set, holds, and at 4–0 Musetti retires, not injured it seems, but embarrassed at being unable to even win a point anymore. What an extraordinary afternoon.

Rafael Nadal then plays Jannik Sinner. The Spaniard is a break down in set one, Sinner serves for the set and is broken quite comfortably by Nadal and things are back on track for a tie-break once more. Nadal then gets going, pounding the young Italian into submission and Nadal, not long after, is 7–5, 4–0 up, the complexion of the match completely changed, predictable once more, and serene for Mr Nadal. Business as usual, you might say. Sinner, to his credit, does not do giving up though. He fights back, wants a respectable scoreline, even if he is going down, and finds his way onto the board, breaking Nadal, and in with a shot. He doesn't manage to recover from being a double break behind and loses the second set 6–3, going down fighting, proud, learning all the time. Nadal again breaks early in the third with no desire to hang around any extra minutes. He delivers Sinner a spirit-breaking bagel, winning 7–5, 6–3, 6–0.

Ukrainian Marta Kostyuk starts to look hot and bothered when she is 1–0 up in set two – having lost the first set 6–3 – and not having any luck on the Iga Świątek serve. That unravelling becomes wholly apparent when Kostyuk is broken to love not long after to go 2–1 down. Świątek is in the ascendency again. Kostyuk takes a tablet for some unknown issue to viewers and breaks straight back. 2–2. A magic pill it might just have proven to be. She knows her moment is close to slipping away and has found something when she needed it. She then holds serve and is leading again at 3–2. Świątek is able to find that special place where the tennis becomes better, stronger, and harder to reply to, and Kostyuk only wins one more game, the Polish defending champion claiming it 6–4 to move into the last eight.

10. The semi-finals beckon for four players today and the story becomes clearer by the day. Some faces fall by the wayside, some surprise names emerge unscathed, and others are those many would have backed from the start.

The quarter-finals kick off with a compelling and, at times bizarre, affair between two new players to this stage of a Grand Slam – Slovenian Tamara Zidanšek and Spaniard Paula Badosa. They break each other for fun, approximately half the games in the match being breaks of service. While each has their ups and downs in a truly topsy-turvy encounter, they are still level at 6–6 in the final set. The difference in such scenarios is just a point here and there, and Zidanšek, serving first, always a game ahead, finds the way to break and clinch the victory and her first ever spot in a major semi-final.

Elena Rybakina hurtles towards her spot taking a 4–1 lead over Anastasia Pavlyuchenkova very quickly. She is also soon pegged back, as in the earlier match, though Rybakina does go on to win the tie-break 7–2. Pavlyuchenkova is good at getting through after losing a set though

– see previous rounds against Sabalenka (R3) and Azárenka (R4) – and she pulls her magic trick off again, winning 9–7 in the final set, and the match has certainly had many traits in common with the earlier quarter-final, taking marginally longer at 2 hours and 33 minutes (the earlier match was 2:26).

The schedule could be messy, but Alexander Zverev solves that by beating Grand Slam quarter-final newcomer Alejandro Davidovich Fokina 6–4, 6–1, 6–1 in an hour and a half – around an hour less than each of the two earlier women's matches.

The showdown between Stefanos Tsitsipas and Daniil Medvedev is the night match. It is a crowd-less spectacle that deserves an audience. Even though the Greek wins in straight sets, Mr Medvedev makes it a contest and proves that his run to this round was no fluke, and he might be able to compete well in future on the surface. He has put to bed the 'no clay courter' theory. Next time, he has to be in the argument. Let us say, for now, that he is a work in progress. At least, he is working on it.

11. **We sort the last players for the semi-final line-up. We are treated to more fascinating encounters, the tennis speaking to us, everything else fading into the background now.**

In the women's quarter-finals, Coco Gauff goes 3–0 up against Barbora Krejčíková, who comes back at her and it is soon 3–3, both players settled and primed for a battle. Krejčíková found some handy aces and Gauff allowed nerves to serve up her usual course of double faults when it mattered.

Gauff breaks again for 5–3, and she then serves for the set. Deuce. Double fault. A miss. Back on serve. It's that simple to lose your way, to watch the tables turn on you. 5–4. Gauff is most nervous when ahead and Krejčíková seems to be edgy when level. But it does culminate in a tie-break, neither pocketing their chances beforehand. What a job Krejčíková made of fighting back twice, thoroughly deserving of a tie-break shot, which she does claim for a one-set lead.

The joy of Krejčíková and the heartbreak of Gauff then swell, spiralling out of control, as Gauff struggles to steady her ship and is soon 5–0 down to her Czech doubles expert opponent. She fights back, remembering to leave it all on court and, after managing to get one break back and have two games on the board, she succumbs to a 7–6, 6–2 defeat. It might hurt, but she will have learned so much from this fortnight.

Iga Świątek – in the last ladies' singles quarter-final – is 2–0 up before you can blink (oddly, every other player who took the early lead in the quarter-final matches ended up losing), and Maria Sakkari soon works her way to 2–2, showing her mettle to level, too. This match is not quite as compelling as the previous ones, 4–4 after 36 minutes, both players unable to ignite at the same time. It isn't pretty and it's yet another shock, as Świątek has an injury issue and is outplayed over two sets, Sakkari emerging victorious, another player to seize the moment and give herself a chance of a major victory in the coming days. It means there will be a new female Grand Slam champion, yet again.

After the last of the women's semi-final spots has been booked, Rafael Nadal takes to the court with Argentine Diego Schwartzman, one of the few players who has come threateningly close in the past to knocking Nadal off his Parisian perch. He rocked it but didn't manage that fatal blow that would see Nadal tumble from on high.

Nadal wins the first set, for 36 back-to-back sets at Roland Garros, but he falters, and Diego wins the second set.

For the first two sets, it looks like Nadal's reign might be in some danger. In set three he gets his moment, seizes it to break, and claims a set that is anything but straightforward, Schwartzman ever posing the Spaniard problems. In set four, Nadal drives home the message that it is still his court, his tournament, his love, and the affair is to continue a little time longer. The match lasts 2 hours and 45 minutes and is precisely what Nadal needed as preparation for the semi-final in which he will likely face his old foe Novak Djokovic.

That he can still find that extra gear and pull away becomes ever more special, as he genuinely appears to be holding back time. Nadal's next match might very well tell us even more.

In the evening, things are anything but Novak Djokovic's way after the first two relatively comfortable sets with his quarter-final opponent Matteo Berrettini finally coming alive and producing some magic. Berrettini wins the third set and pushes all the way in the fourth. However, Djokovic claims a night-session win to an empty arena after they had to pause proceedings to remove the audience because the Paris curfew of 11:00 pm was passed during the match.

12. The women's semi-finals give us a glimpse of the stunning depth of the women's game.

Looking ahead to tomorrow's men's semi-final – for the Grand Slam tally, the final number count, episode number 58 of the ongoing and extraordinary Nadal–Djokovic saga is perhaps the most important of them all. Should the winner go on to claim the title, Nadal would pull three majors clear of Djokovic and one of Federer atop the list, or Djokovic would get to within one of equalling Federer and Nadal's tallies of 20 each.

History, as ever with the pair, is on the line. It cannot be understated what spectacular tennis the meeting between the two men is likely to bring out in each of them yet again. These are not mere tennis matches but Herculean battles of gods, men greater than mortals, which will be relived, replayed, and revisited for decades to come.

The first ladies' semi sees Tamara Zidanšek 2–0 up before Anastasia Pavlyuchenkova bursts into life and it becomes 3–2. The Russian is 5–3 and serving for the set a short while later and, after a couple of chances, Zidanšek gets things back on serve at 5–4. She will serve next to stay in a compelling first set. You can't take your eyes off this one.

Serving at 5–6 down, Zidanšek buckles and Pavlyuchenkova breaks – before a tie-break is called for – and takes the opener. The second set does offer Zidanšek a way back when she breaks after losing serve, but it soon sees Zidanšek broken for a second time immediately after for the Russian to then serve her way successfully into a first major final.

Maria Sakkari breaks in the first game of her following semi-final with Barbora Krejčíková. The break is retrieved in only the next game, and the players are pushing and pulling, attempting to find a gap to jump into, seeking a way to get ahead, neck and neck as they go – break and be broken.

Krejčíková is 3–1 down, almost 4–1. She doesn't panic and it's 3–2. Soon she has made it 5–3, heading into the distance, serving for the opening set. But the curse of recent women's matches sees her at 0–30 and broken shortly afterwards. 5–5. The Czech finds the way through, breaks, and then holds and takes it 7–5.

Sakkari storms through the first half of set two and gets to 4–0. The match tos and fros. The Czech player comes back but, ultimately, the double break proved too much to recover from and the Greek wins the second set 6–4 and forces what will be a compelling decider. When serving for the match and a place in the final, Sakkari faces a break point. Sakkari hits a winner and gets to deuce. The match clock shows 2:42.

Another turnaround ensues when Krejčíková gets into the lead, at 6–5, in the final set. Sakkari serves to stay alive and keeps her nose level, a photo finish impossible, and yet nothing separating the pair still. At 6–7 down, Sakkari serves again to keep her hopes of reaching a first major final alive, but this time faces two match points at 15–40. This, however, is the match that keeps on giving and at deuce, moments later, Krejčíková gets a net cord that brings up a third match point. Sakkari gets a rare ace to restore the score to deuce, and on we go …

Two games later, at 7–8, Sakkari faces match point again. Krejčíková thinks Sakkari's shot is out and that she has won. The umpire comes down to inspect the ball mark and proclaims it in. Replay the point, ladies. Sakkari has lived to strike another ball in this match. She saves it again. Four match points now saved. The next one is unmistakably won by Krejčíková. It's a devastating match to lose and Sakkari will be heartbroken after coming so close. For Krejčíková it is cloud nine and a final spot for two days from now. The match ends with 3:18 on the clock, somewhat surprisingly.

13. Thrilling men's semi-final's day

Stefanos Tsitsipas gets an early break from which Alexander Zverev doesn't recover in set one. Things then switch, and the Greek slips to 0–3 down in the second, before forging a way back and getting to 5–3 up with several return breaks of the German's serve.

The second set culminates with Tsitsipas winning his sixth game in a row to complete a wonderful turnaround and see the Greek camp joyous. It isn't over, but it's a fantastic lead. He's heading for his maiden major final if he doesn't implode here. We are in for a spectacular match as Zverev locates his best tennis, his finest work, and wins the next two sets with crucial breaks and clinical serving.

Zverev then has a chance in the deciding set. At 0–40 he gets three shots at a vital break. He cannot take any of them. Tsitsipas then does and the Greek gets to 5–2, doesn't quite break to take the match and then serves for a place in his first Grand Slam final – against the experience of either Rafael Nadal or Novak Djokovic.

Match point number five is on Tsitsipas's own serve, and he clinches that magical final berth with an ace.

Following that comes the one everyone has been waiting for – the centrepiece of the day, perhaps the whole tournament: Nadal v Djokovic.

Rafa would become the oldest man to reach the Roland Garros men's final in the open era, at 35. It is the pair's fifty-eighth meeting, the ninth at Roland Garros. Nadal leads that head-to-head 7–1.

Is it the match with the greatest meaning ever? The most loaded significance of all?

Nadal faces two break points in the opening game, which he escapes from with an ace and a serve Djokovic can only just get the frame on, sending it far from the court. Even the first game feels like a battle within a war. It is 10 minutes before Nadal can finally hold. What an opening! We are in for a treat.

At 5–1 to Nadal, he has a wobble, and faces two break points. He saves them. He can't seal the set shut and must face another break point. This time the Serb breaks. 5–0 has become 5–2.

Djokovic saves a break point and holds serve for 5–3, fighting every inch. The swirling marks of the court look ready to swallow somebody up. The crowd is well and truly gripped. Nadal crosses the first set finishing line for 6–3.

At 1–0 down in the second set, Nadal throws in a terrible service game and is broken, the pressure from his opponent relentless. He is 2–0 down and has won only one of the last six games. A real shift has taken place.

0–40. Nadal immediately breaks back to love. 2–1. Djokovic gets another break though and soon leads 4–2. Break points are the holy grail. One of the pair's infamous, epic rallies ensues deeper into the set, ending with Nadal hitting into the net, Djokovic simply outlasting as he does so well. Deuce again. The moment is huge for the entire match, a wrestle for the power taking place before our eyes.

Djokovic has Nadal pushed to his absolute limit. It's that visible. Nadal hits the most extraordinary winner from a losing position that you will ever see, and he gets to break-back point to keep the set alive. Once more. He cannot convert. He gets another though. These are *the* chances. Everyone is now on the edge of their seats. It's uneasy, nerve-wracking for all involved, and the hitting is as big as has ever been seen, surely. Nadal doesn't get things back on terms and Djokovic levels the match at one set all.

My wife says it is like a boxing match, and nothing could be more accurate at this stage.

Djokovic gets a break in the third, Nadal gets it back, but then loses his service game to love and the Serbian world number one leads 4–3 and will serve next. 5–3. He's starting to pull away from Nadal, out-mastering the Spanish clay court genius.

It's almost impossible to write, so breath-taking is the tennis taking place right now. 5–4 and Djokovic serves for the set. How do these men always fashion chances when their backs are against the wall? Nadal breaks back on the first break point and it's 5–5. As Nadal draws level, the crowd behind him jumps out of its seats as one and goes utterly bonkers.

As the saga continues, both men are pumped and howling after winning points like we have only ever seen at their most animal-esque moments. These are not mere tennis players; these men are superheroes.

Nadal retains a service hold and will then have a crack at breaking the Serbian serve to take the third set, which a little while ago had looked near impossible. This set is likely the key to the match, and Djokovic is an expert at forcing essential tie-breaks.

A 92-minute set, that any loser on earth would likely not recover from losing, a masterpiece of a set, one that defies belief in what is humanly possible in sport, ends with Djokovic winning it 7–4. Just tougher and less error-prone when it most counts. The match clock after the third set reads 3:33.

It's hard to think anyone could last, at this level, if it went to a full five sets. That third set was probably decisive and would surely have broken anyone of Nadal's age, even the greatest clay court player ever. Rafa, though, starts well and breaks, holds and is soon at 2–0. But the breaks are coming thick and fast again as Nadal is broken and it's 2–2. Novak then surges, having retrieved a break that was surely vital for Nadal to retain at the start of the set. Rafa looks tired, broken, defeated. Novak doesn't look back as he wins six games in a row and, finally, Nadal is shuffled out of his beloved Parisian event. The Serb claims a famous victory over Nadal.

It finishes after 11:15 pm. It has quite simply been mind-bending tennis. From another planet, galaxy, universe? Yes, that stratosphere only these two men know.

14. The ladies' final is contested, now rather unsurprisingly, by two first-timers – who have never met before – in 29-year-old Russian Anastasia Pavlyuchenkova and 25-year-old doubles-specialist Czech (what a startling wealth of riches in Czech women's tennis!) Barbora Krejčíková. It is indeed an intriguing encounter.

Krejčíková has a frighteningly nervy start and loses her serve. She then relaxes and goes on a confident run of games that takes her to 5–1 and sees her serve for an almost dream-like first set at around the half-hour mark. A place with the greats of the game beckons here, and Krejčíková has played the first set fittingly. 6–1, and she's halfway there. It is worth considering how Pavlyuchenkova has won multiple matches this fortnight after being a set down. Krejčíková is patient, calm, saves two early break points at 0–40, but the Russian seizes her chance on the third one and gets ahead 2–0. When Pavlyuchenkova is 5–1 up, now breaking for fun, and serving for the set, the 1-hour mark is hit as the score shows 30–30.

Pavlyuchenkova then gets a set point. It is saved. Deuce. Break point Krejčíková. Deuce. The Czech does break and then the Russian takes an injury time-out at 5–2 up. She has her left thigh bandaged and play resumes. She eventually breaks Krejčíková – for 6–2 – and we are headed for a deciding set in the ladies' singles final after around 70 minutes of play.

One set. No tie-break. The winner of it gets the trophy and a first major title.

Krejčíková leaves the court for far too long again – a trick she has perfected – and she is endearing herself to nobody with such shenanigans. Players sometimes need to leave the tennis court. Absolutely they do. This however is making a mockery of that. To leave the court regularly, as a tactic, and be gone for so long is disrespectful to the opponent, the crowd, and the sport itself.

Final set. Finally, we get underway, and first blood goes to Krejčíková when she breaks for 2–1. She serves next, but at 0–40, Pavlyuchenkova has three bites at the cherry to importantly get that break straight back. Two are saved and the third is pounced on with a brilliant winner. 2–2. 3–2. The Russian noses back in front. Krejčíková with an easy service game to love (the kind you dream of at this stage of proceedings in such a big match), and there is nothing to separate the pair in the final set. 3–3.

Krejčíková, however, has other ideas, turns on her best tennis at the crucial moment and gets to 0–40 for three chances at a timely break. She takes the very first with arguably her best game of hitting the whole match, seeing the ball like a beachball. 4–3. She will serve to be within only one game.

30–30. Krejčíková is the braver of the pair, going for her shots, getting to game point. It would be a huge hold. Into the net. Deuce. Advantage Krejčíková after a blinding serve that did not find its way back into the court. She does hold. 5–3. The Czech, the two-time doubles major winner, is only a game away from a maiden Grand Slam singles title.

15–40. Pavlyuchenkova saves two break points that are also match and championship points. Deuce. Two points later it is 5–4, the Russian keeping it alive. Next comes the truest test of a player's bottle – Krejčíková will have to serve for the biggest win of her career.

Efficient stuff from the Czech and it's 15–0. A shot into the net undoes the good start. Beautiful attacking tennis from Krejčíková gets her to 30–15, two points away. No sign of nerves. She hits another beautiful winner, moving Pavlyuchenkova all around the baseline, and has two match points. Fault. Double fault. Tension, finally. Is it going to tell right at the last? One more …

The fourth match point however is the final one as Barbora Krejčíková joins the pantheon of legends, of ladies' Roland Garros singles title winners. A truly surprising story and the women's tour just cannot stop providing us with new Grand Slam champions.

15. For the second men's major final of 2021 a young pretender to the Grand Slam throne will take on the best player in the world, Novak Djokovic. This time, it is Stefanos Tsitsipas's chance to see if he can topple the Serbian master as he attempts to get within one of the tallies of Roger and Rafa.

The first set reaches a tie-break in which Tsitsipas finds himself in the rather spiffing position of being 4–0 up. He serves at 5–6 though to stay in the set, after having had a missed set point on the Djokovic serve (when Tsitsipas led the set 5–4). Tsitsipas survives that one against him and pockets the first set 8–6 on the tie-break.

Tsitsipas goes on to break Djokovic comfortably in the first game of the second set.

In this bright sunlight and heat, Nadal would probably have beaten Djokovic. Djokovic likes the cooler conditions like the evening match with Nadal two days earlier. The weather today suits Tsitsipas more and it is showing. He breaks the world number one's serve twice and leads by two sets to love, much to the surprise of many watching.

Djokovic then comes back, breaks the Greek, and continues to hold his own serve. Has there ever been anyone as solid and unbeatable as the Serbian? At 2–5, Tsitsipas successfully serves to stay in the third set. Djokovic seals the set shut 6–3 a game later.

Djokovic then wins the fourth set 6–2, levels the match, and stuns Tsitsipas.

The shadow of the stand and its flags starts to move across the court. At 1–1 it is almost halfway on the court, affecting things, posing new problems for the players. But Novak Djokovic did not come back from being down two sets to love – fighting for his substantial slice of history – to then lose in the final set to a rookie finalist.

It is done and dusted when Djokovic gets an early break for 2–1 in the final set and manages to stay ahead, serving for it at 5–4 and completing a masterful comeback. He is just made for these occasions and now owns 19 Grand Slam titles. He could draw level with the other two greatest players ever in a month's time at Wimbledon (and he does indeed go on to do just that). Only a fool would ever bet against the Serb.

JUST BEFORE WIMBLEDON KICKS OFF
JUNE 2021

When Roger Met Félix

The pair – Roger Federer and Félix Auger-Aliassime – separated by several tennis-playing generations share a birthday (only 19 years between the two men), and today sees their first ever match together (on grass) at fabled Federer's beloved Halle Open in Germany.

Something about the brilliance of the surely soon-to-be-outgoing hero of tennis, Federer, meeting a bright, young hope of the game in Auger-Aliassime – and a pair sharing a star sign (if you follow all that jazz) and birthday in common – is well worth contemplating.

Roger is tuning up. Is it for one last assault on the Wimbledon men's singles title? Or does he have more in the tank to see him into 2022?

The game of Félix looks glorious on grass (after rather a tame and disappointing clay court season). He looks a natural. While he loses the opening set to the master of the green turf, he does find his feet, the ones that brought him a runner-up place in last week's Stuttgart grass court tournament, and he outplays Federer in the second and third sets to win and possess a 1–0 head-to-head with the man who has undeniably played the most beautiful tennis many have ever seen. 4–6, 6–3, 6–2.

Félix is a player of now and the future. If he keeps on getting better, who knows what he can go on to accomplish. One thing is for sure, he is going to be lodged inside that top 10, soon, alongside Dominic

Thiem, Daniil Medvedev, Alexander Zverev, Stefanos Tsitsipas, Matteo Berrettini, and Andrey Rublev (and the other 20-somethings when the Big Three finally head towards the exit).

Grass Is Go!

Nothing is surprising anymore as we push on playing, watching, and wondering about the world of tennis in the midst of a global pandemic. The event of minor but well-known grass court events happening (in Nottingham and Stuttgart) during the French Open – the clay court finale – is unusual to say the least. Attention shifts to grass quickly, but with Roland Garros having been delayed by a week, the usual three-week gap between the end of one major in Paris and the next on grass at Wimbledon is hardly in need of being shortened, again (as it was until only a few years ago).

The lawns of tennis, the stripes from the perfect trimming by grass experts, the orange, or is it red of the clay courts, become a mere memory now. If summer never quite seems to last long enough as we outdoor creatures revel in the sunshine and conditions, it is reflected in the racing by of the summer window of sport.

Ah! Those fresh green lawns. They speak to us of summer in all its exquisite glory. Those immaculately kept, nurtured, loved lawns, those courts have something – along with their freshly painted white lines – that no other tennis surface has. They age before our eyes over the week or fortnight during which the action graces those courts.

They reveal different sides in different conditions, nuances of character, not to mention as the sun plays with the obstructions throwing shades upon the court, an extra obstacle for players to surmount.

The Last Chance Saloon

Wimbledon 2021 is surely the last chance saloon for Serena Williams and Roger Federer and their hopes of adding further major title glory to their vast collections. It may appear too clinical an observation, but sentiment will not protect them further. Not just age is a factor, but the younger players who are now able to prevail, who have been jostling and nudging and even barging them out of the way, are increasingly stealing their spotlight.

Will the legends be fit? Will they be able to hurt the players that have damaged their chances of adding to their major silverware tallies in recent years? Will they get the luck of the draw and see their puzzles falling into place? And will they find their best tennis, once again, when they need it the most and move towards the heart of the battle, the rounds they are dying to get their teeth into? One thing is for sure, they will be there, ever ready to pounce, to take advantage of any weakness others may have, and to extend their colossal and simply beautiful legacies. They really should take a bow.